FROM
WHERE YOU
DREAM

FROM WHERE YOU DREAM

THE PROCESS OF WRITING FICTION

Robert Olen Butler

EDITED WITH AN INTRODUCTION BY
Janet Burroway

Grove Press
New York

Portions of this book previously appeared in
The Writer's Chronicle and *Five Points*.

Published simultaneously in Canada
Printed in the United States of America

FIRST EDITION

Library of Congress Cataloging-in-Publication Data
Butler, Robert Olen.
From where you dream : the process of writing fiction / Robert Olen Butler ; edited, with an introduction by Janet Burroway.
p. cm.
ISBN 0-8021-1795-3
1. Fiction—Authorship.   I. Burroway, Janet.   II. Title.
808.3—dc22   2005040251

Grove Press
an imprint of Grove/Atlantic, Inc.
841 Broadway
New York, NY 10003

05 06 07 08 09 10 9 8 7 6 5 4 3 2 1

ACKNOWLEDGMENTS

Many people helped shape the insights in this book, and I am deeply grateful. For the pioneering faculty of Northwestern University's Oral Interpretation department—Wallace Bacon, Lilla Heston, Charlotte Lee, and particularly Robert Breen. There is no better undergraduate training for a nascent writer than Oral Interpretation, now called in university speech departments "Performance Studies." For my friend and teacher and mentor, Anatole Broyard. For my father, Robert Olen Butler, Sr., who taught me the essentials and nurtured the rest, and my son, Joshua Butler, for all the wonderful hours exploring the nature of narrative together. For my wife, Elizabeth Dewberry, who has profoundly influenced how I see everything. And a special debt of gratitude to Janet Burroway for her brilliant fiction, her extraordinary text on writing, and her friendship. If she had not graciously taken on the work of editing my lectures into a book, my aesthetic philosophy never would have found expression outside my own classroom.

Janet and I would both like to thank the students of Florida State University who contributed their short stories and exercise results to this volume and Nikki Louis for her invaluable help with the preparation of the manuscript.

—Robert Olen Butler

CONTENTS

To supplement his lectures on creative writing, Robert Olen Butler undertook, in the fall of 2001, an Internet project to demonstrate the creative process. In seventeen, two-hour, real-time webcasts he created a short story from first conception to final, polished manuscript. This event remains archived at www.fsu.edu/butler.

INTRODUCTION

Sometime in the early 1980s, the playwright Maria Irene Fornes came to Florida State University to conduct a series of workshops. I had already been teaching writing for a decade and had published a book on *Writing Fiction*, and I was disconcerted, not to say traumatized, by her methods. She had us do calisthenics, pair up and draw portraits of each other, imagine the insides of our stomachs and set play scenes there. At the end of the last session, I told her, "I've spent twenty years understanding my process, and you're asking me to change it entirely."

Fornes bounced her palms at the air. "You must always keep changing your process!" she declared. "Because there are two of you, one who wants to write and one who doesn't. The one who wants to write has to keep fooling the one who doesn't."

I have taken her advice to heart and have tried to keep changing—expanding, twisting, tricking—my writing process, but the truth is that only two teachers have radically changed it for me. One was Fornes, and the other is Robert Olen Butler, who joined the FSU faculty in 2000 as Eppes Professor of Creative Writing. Butler's method is largely lecture—his students do not draw, dance, or gather in small groups—yet his teaching, like Fornes's, offers a door into the unconscious where fiction lies.

Butler's background is in theater—he trained in both acting and oral interpretation and began his professional career as an actor—and what he often calls "method writing" owes much to the director Konstantin Stanislavsky of the Moscow Art Theatre, who revolutionized dramatic practice for the twentieth century and, in effect, made possible the emotional realism of film. The so-called Stanislavsky Method rests on two principles: that the actor's body is an instrument that must be supple, strong, and prepared; and that craft is always secondary to the truth of emotional connection. Both of these principles have their counterpart in Butler's teaching of the fictional process. In place of the body, it is the imagination that must be a strong and supple instrument, ready to lead the reader through moment-by-moment sensual experience. And it is in the realm of the unconscious rather than that of technique or intellect that the writer seeks fictional truth.

I attended Butler's graduate fiction course in the fall of 2001, took copious notes, began applying his advice to my own work, and proposed—because he will not set non-fictional pen to paper—that I would get the lectures out in the world. In the fall of 2002 I attended again while Butler wore a minirecorder to tape his talks. These were (impeccably) transcribed by graduate writer Nikki Louis, and then I set to work to edit them. The lectures are delivered extempore from five three-by-five cards from which Butler picks almost at random. Consequently, in the editing I have cut and shuffled, sometimes incorporating the answer to a student question where it fits into the body of the text. I've tried to snip the ravelings,

expunge the repetitions, and sift out the *er-uh* factor of im-
promptu speech while leaving the informality and energy intact. It's a task closer to proofreading than to translating, but
involving a little of both.

As Butler frequently points out, his lectures are necessarily the inverse of his advice; he generalizes, analyzes, and ab-
stracts as a way of inveighing against generalization, analysis,
and abstraction. His self-declared obsessions have to do with
the descent into the dreamspace of the unconscious in order to
discover the yearning that is at the center of every person and
therefore of every character, and with the moment-to-
moment sensual experiencing of that character's story. He proposes fiction as the exploration of the human condition and
yearning as its compass. He conducts exercises to achieve the
dreamspace. He offers insights into the nature of voice. He is
eloquent on fiction as a "cinema of the mind," to be experienced
by the reader as a sensual series of takes and scenes. And he has
devised a system whereby revision is undertaken at the level of
structure rather than sentence.

Many practitioners and teachers of writing (myself included) have preached freewriting, clustering, drafting, and
generally "making clay"—getting any words whatsoever on the
page, in order to have material to work with. Butler's writing
"zone" is instead a place of meditation on the sense experience of the characters, requiring both patience and a depth of
concentration that must be surrendered to and cannot be
willed.

Yet over and over again, in modes practical and inspiring,
Butler's perspective has helped me to my own best writing. In

a 1978 journal that turned up as part of Janet Sternburg's an-
thology, *The Writer on Her Work*, I complained that "the grind,
the shit, of fiction, is the need to shape and construct. Letters
flow from me. I always intend to let a novel do the same; every
time I promise myself that I'll do a quick imperfect draft . . .
But I can't do so. These three days have yielded six pages, plus
an opening about opening *The Opening* that I scrapped
entirely. And that are imperfect by a long shot yet. Decisions
have to be made in them—about character, the focus of the
reader's anticipation, tone—that make it impossible to pro-
ceed until the decisions are made." Butler's "dangerous system"
of novel construction addresses precisely this perennial problem of the draft writer and offers a way out. It allows the
simultaneous emergence of structure, character, and motif.
The system is primarily intended for the novel, but I have
found it, for both short stories and plays, a way to bypass the
gnarled intellectual process that had marred my "plotting."

Because in the pursuit of sensual truth Butler so often
dismisses concept and abstraction, it's a pleasurable paradox
to find in these lectures thoughtful and original perspectives
on ideas that touch science, psychology, and other arts. The
"five ways of experiencing emotion" outlined in chapter one—
about which Butler has been casually holding forth for nearly
twenty years—correspond directly to the neural research analyzed in Antonio Damasio's 1999 *The Feeling of What Happens*.
His discussion of the writer in search of his form describes the
struggle in Gabriel Josipovici's classic essay on Nathaniel
Hawthorne in *The World and the Book*. His analysis of Dickens

as moviemaker illustrates and elaborates D. W. Griffith's perception on that subject.

I have to say that, as with Fornes, my initial resistance to Butler's message was strong. His central obsessions lead him toward words about which I am preternaturally squeamish—like *dream* and *unconscious* and *trance* and *yearning* and *white-hot center* and *art object*—whereas I have been known to describe myself as a *contriver*, which would certainly make him squirm. I am fascinated by the intricacies of craft, which Butler assures me are a distraction. I have a crusading high regard for intellect, whereas he insists that as a fiction writer I must not "think."

In the teaching continuum from therapist to maestro, Butler is definitely in the camp of the maestro. I once assigned a graduate class Annie Dillard's *The Writing Life*—a book I love—and one of the students said, "It's so effing high-minded it makes me want to go to the Kmart." Butler is effing high-minded. He is an enthusiast, demanding and prescriptive. But his lectures also exhilarate. They respect your reach.

JB

PART ONE

THE LECTURES

1

BOOT CAMP

"To be an artist means never to avert your eyes."
—Akira Kurosawa

I need to make this clear first off: no matter where you are in your writing career, if you aspire to create literature, if you aspire to be an artist in the medium of language, if you aspire to create narratives of whatever length that arrive at the condition of art—there are fundamental truths about the artistic process to which you must attend.

In the nearly two decades I've been teaching this subject, I have read many thousands of manuscripts from aspiring writers, and virtually all of them—virtually *all* of them—fail to show an intuitive command of the essentials of the process of fictional art. Because of the creative writing pedagogy in this country, and because of the nature of this art form, and because of the medium you work with, and because of the rigors of artistic vision, and because of youth, and because no one has ever told you these things clearly, the great likelihood is that all of the fiction you've written is mortally flawed in terms of the essentials of process.

This, I think, is why my students have come to call this boot camp: because—and I will do this in as friendly and gentle and encouraging a way as I possibly can—what I have to say to you will indict virtually everything you've written.

It's not going to be an easy message to hear. But I'm going to tell you right up front: before I wrote my first published novel, *The Alleys of Eden*, I wrote literally a million words of absolute dreck. Five god-awful novels, forty dreadful short stories, and a dozen truly terrible full-length plays. I made all those fatal errors of process I would bet my mortgage you're making now. I want to help you get around that. But you've got to open up and listen to me about this. If you're not prepared to do that, if you're not prepared to open your sensibilities—and, incidentally, your minds—to what I'm going to tell you and to the implications for the work you have done and will do, then it is best that you and I part ways now. There are some folks in this room who will attest to the fact that it's going to be tough, it's going to be nerve-racking, it's going to unsettle you. But I think they will also attest that the rewards are worth it.

You must, to be in here, have the highest aspirations for yourselves as writers—the desire to create works of fiction that will endure, that reflect and articulate the deepest truth about the human condition. If that is your aspiration, then this is where you belong. I will not blow you off. I will take your aspirations seriously, and I will demand that you take them seriously.

I always begin with something the great Japanese film director Akira Kurosawa once said. He said, "To be an artist means never to avert your eyes." To be an artist means never to avert your eyes—this is the absolute essential truth here.

You're going to be, and probably always have been, led to avert your eyes. But turning from that path is what it means to be an artist. You need courage, and that's something I can't teach you. I *can* teach you that you've got to have it.

What does an artist do?

As an artist, like everyone else on this planet, you encounter the world out there primarily in your bodies, moment to moment through your senses. Everything else derives from that. You are creatures of your senses. All that follows—all the stuff of the mind, all the analysis, all the rationalization, all the abstracting and interpreting—follows upon that point of contact, in the moment, through your senses.

If you live in the moment, through your senses, your first impression certainly will be that at the heart of things is chaos. God knows we had a very clear example of that in September of 2001. You can be sitting on the ninetieth floor of the World Trade Center on a beautiful late summer morning, smelling your Starbucks coffee, glad they brewed Sumatra today, and someone with visions of seventy-two virgins waiting for him in heaven flies a United Airlines jet through your window. That is a paradigm of the human condition.

Artists are intensely aware of the chaos implied by the moment-to-moment sensual experience of human beings on this planet. But they also, paradoxically, have an intuition that behind the chaos there is meaning; behind the flux of moment-to-moment experience there is a deep and abiding order.

The artist shares her intuition of the world's order with the philosophers, the theologians, the scientists, the psychoanalysts—there are lots of people who believe there is order in the universe—but those others embrace the understanding and expression of that order through abstractions, through ideas, through analytical thought. The artist is deeply uncomfortable with those modes of understanding and expression. The theologians have their dogma and the philosophers their theories and the scientists their scientific principles and the psychoanalysts their Jungian or Freudian insights—but to those modes of expression and understanding the artist says, "That doesn't make sense to me. Those are not the terms in which I intuit the world." The artist cannot understand or access her vision of the world in any of those ways. The artist is comfortable only with going back to the way in which the chaos is first encountered—that is, moment to moment through the senses. Then, selecting from that sensual moment-to-moment experience, picking out bits and pieces of it, reshaping it, she recombines it into an object that a reader in turn encounters as if it were experience itself: a record of moment-to-moment sensual experience, an encounter as direct as those we have with life itself. Only in this way, by shaping and ordering experience into an art object, is the artist able to express her deep intuition of order.

There's an interesting precedent for this idea—and what I'm about to observe has no intended religious message. A very influential person in Western and world culture taught almost exclusively in one way: only by parable, by telling stories. "Without a parable he spake not unto them." He asked questions similar to the ones I just suggested artists ask: What is the abiding universal human condition? What is this all about here on planet Earth? And his answer was, *There was a guy who owned a vineyard and he had a son . . .* and so forth. He told stories. That's what was clearly recorded in the books written closest to the time in which Jesus of Nazareth lived. Jesus said, emphatically, "He that hath ears to hear, let him hear." He did not say, "He that hath a brain to think, let him think." It's through the ear. By means of a story.

The great jazz trumpeter Miles Davis said, "Man, you don't play what you know, you play what you hear." Davis had very strong political ideas—but he was an artist; he knew that you don't make music from ideas.

Please get out of the habit of saying that you've got an *idea* for a short story. Art does not come from ideas. Art does not come from the mind. Art comes from the place where you dream. Art comes from your unconscious; it comes from the white-hot center of you.

Does this make sense? Do you understand what I'm saying? If you want to think your way into your fiction, if you think you can analyze your way into a work of art, we're going to be totally at odds philosophically about what art is and where it comes from. But if you have this aspiration and an open sensibility, and if what I'm saying makes sense, then you have to tell your mind to back the hell off. It's another place in yourself entirely where you must look to create a work of art. And I'll wager that virtually everything you've written so far has come from your head.

You know, it's easy to get caught up in the ambition of being a writer. It's easy to get caught up in loving literature and wishing to be the person on the dust jacket. This ambition, as innocent-seeming as it is, can very easily muscle out your deeper, more delicate, more difficult ambitions. It can muscle them out in favor of: *I want to get published, I want to be famous, I want to win a prize.* Or even in the terms: *I want to be an artist.* I said earlier, "If you aspire to *create* art." Please understand that's different from "I want to *be* a great artist." And even "I want to create art" is a bit of a dangerous ambition. What I want to nurture in you is the impulse: "I'm ravished by sensual experience. I yearn to take life in. My God! I've got this sense that the world has meaning. Things roil around in my dream space, and I've got to figure out how to make art objects of them." That's really the best ambition, to be hungry for sensual experience in your life. Ravenous. Artists are not intellectuals. We are sensualists. The objects we create are sensual objects, and the way you'll know that you're writing from your head is that you'll look at your story and find it full of abstraction and generalization and summary and analysis and interpretation. These modes of discourse will be prevalent in works that are written from the head. Even if you can by force of will insert some nicely observed sense details into the work, you'll find the work moving toward analysis and description and generalization and abstraction when, in fact, in the work of art the most important moments are the most sensual of all, the most in the moment.

Mies van der Rohe said that God is in the details. Let's substitute: the human condition resides in the details, the sense details.

The primary point of contact for the reader is going to be an emotional one, because *emotions reside in the senses*. What we do with emotions after that, to protect ourselves in the world, is a different thing; but emotions are experienced in the senses and therefore are best expressed in fiction through the senses.

Emotions are also basically experienced, and therefore expressed in fiction, in five ways. First, we have a sensual reaction inside our body—temperature, heartbeat, muscle reaction, neural change.

Second, there is a sensual response that sends signals outside of our body—posture, gesture, facial expression, tone of voice, and so forth.

Third, we have, as an experience of emotion, flashes of the past. Moments of reference in our past come back to us in our consciousness, not as ideas or analyses about the past, but as little vivid bursts of waking dream; they come back as images, sense impressions.

The fourth way we experience emotion and can therefore express it in fiction is that there are flashes of the future, similar to flashes of the past, but of something that has not yet happened or that may happen, something we desire or fear or otherwise anticipate. Those also come to us as images, like bursts of waking dreams.

And finally—this is important for the fiction writer— we experience what I would call sensual selectivity. At any given moment we, and therefore our characters, are surrounded by hundreds and hundreds of sensual cues. But in that moment only a very small number of those sensual cues will impinge on our consciousness. Now, what makes that selection for us? Well, our emotions do.

Henry James said that "landscape is character," and this could well be what he meant. Our personalities, our emotions, are expressed in response to the sensual cues around us. We look at the landscape and what we see out there is our deepest emotional inner selves. This is at the heart of a work of art.

Why is this sensual center of our art so hard for us to get at? Miles Davis, if he were a writer, probably would struggle with the same problems I struggled with and that you're probably struggling with now. It's easy for him to say "you don't play what you know, you play what you hear," because his medium is entirely sensual, inescapably so. The sound that comes out of his horn is irreducibly sensual. Every other art form is irreducibly sensual. Dancers move, composers work with sound, painters with color; even abstract art isn't abstract at all—it's color and form. You stand in front of a Barnett Newman painting, and whatever may have been in his brain about artistic theory, what confronts you is a massive experience of color and a delicate experience of texture.

But you folks have it really difficult. No one in my position in any of the other arts has to say the things I say. Why? Because your medium is language, and language is not innately sensual. Language, in fact, is much more often used in non-sensual ways. Look at the paradox of this evening. I am inveighing against abstraction, generalization, and summary and analysis and interpretation in what terms? Abstract, general, analytical, and interpretive. Am I not? Well, that's the nature of human beings. There are things we have to express in this way.

Now, I've heard no gasps of recognition yet, but let me assume that some of you are thinking, Of course, this makes sense. Oh boy oh boy! If so, you and I are still going to have to be patient, because—you know what?—your understanding is still here in your head, and it's going to take a while to make all this part of your process.

If I had me to talk to me back when, I might not have had to write a million dreadful words. If I'd caught me at the right moment—and in the right spirit—I might have had to write only a *quarter* of a million—maybe not so many as that if I'd really listened. You might ask, why did he write *five* terrible novels? How many terrible novels can you write? The answer is that I had no idea how badly I was writing. None. And my ability to continue working through a million words was so rooted in self-deception that I might not have been able to hear this message. So those are the things you may have to sort through, too.

The special problem here is that the artistic medium of fiction writers—language—is not innately sensual. The medium is unforgiving whenever we look for it in our minds. Some visual artists do a lot of conceptualizing and still end up creating terrific works of art. They are able to do so because once they get out there in front of their canvases or their blocks of granite, they have to leave those ideas behind. The medium itself won't let them think.

Literature—language, fiction—does not as a medium force you to leave your ideas behind. And if you think it into being, if you will a story into being, by God, it's going to show.

Why is it so tough to get past that? Why does Kurosawa say that the essence of being an artist is that you can't avert your eyes? Why avert them? We still haven't quite made that connection. If the artist sees the chaos of experience and feels order behind it and creates objects to express that order, surely that is reassuring, right? Well, at some point maybe. But what do you have to do first? And why is it so hard? This is why—and this is why virtually all inexperienced writers end up in their heads instead of the unconscious: because the unconscious is scary as hell. It *is* hell for many of us.

If I say art doesn't come from the mind, it comes from the place where you dream, you may say, "Well, I wake up screaming in the night. I don't want to go into my dreams, thank you very much. I don't want to go into that white-hot center; I've spent my life staying out of there. That's why I'm sitting in this classroom, why I was able to draw a comb through my hair this morning. Because I haven't gone there, I don't go there. I've got lots of ways of staying out of there." And you know what? You still need those ways twenty-one or twenty-two hours a day. But this is the tough part: for those two hours a day when you write, you cannot flinch. You have to go down into that deepest, darkest, most roiling, white-hot place—it can't be white-hot and dark at the same time, but I don't care—that paradox, live with it—whatever scared the hell out of you down there—and there's plenty—you have to go in there; down into the deepest part of it, and you can't flinch, can't walk away. That's the only way to create a work of art—even though you have plenty of defense mechanisms to keep you out of there, and those defense mechanisms are going to work against you mightily.

I fight this battle every day. Janet fights this battle every day. Every artist in the world fights this battle every day. To go to a scary place that makes some other part of you say: *What are you doing? No. Just no. No. No.* Your hands are poised over the keyboard, and that voice says, *Look at your fingernails; they need clipping.* And when the voice has got you in the bathroom: *Look at the toilet; it needs cleaning.* And you say, *Yes! Anything, anything but to go back and face this stuff.*

Not only that. That voice wants to draw you up into your head. And you know what that head has been for you all your life? Everyone in this room, I'm sure, has been significantly smarter in all kinds of ways than the people around you. You've had your own view of things, and you haven't really followed the crowd, because you're a little too smart for that—or way too smart—and you see things in a different way. You're isolated. And in order to get through childhood and puberty and adolescence and young adulthood, broken relationships and a marriage or two, or four—you have identified with your mind. *I'm smart, I'm smarter than they are.* There's a part of your mind you've been rewarded for all through school, and that is your literal memory. You'll be rewarded for it again in classrooms in this same program. You remember things; you can talk these things back and command details. You know literature. You've always found your self-worth there, and what I'm telling you is that literal memory is your enemy. It's been a large part of your identity all your life, and that part is going to want to drag you down, to destroy the things you create. That's not an easy message to take.

Furthermore, you've got this self-conscious metavoice going all the time. I do, and I'm sure a lot of you do, too. You sit quietly and your metavoice is talking to you in your head. "Well, here I'm sitting," it says. And even, "OK, maybe I shouldn't think so much now. That sounds like it's something I probably should try, to see if I can do that." These words are going through your head, right? This is going on all the time; there's all this analytical garbage running through your mind. This self-conscious metavoice; it's a voice about the voice. It's like talking about my own consciousness.

This is why Catholics and Muslims have repetitive, predetermined prayers, why the Hindus and the Zen Buddhists and the Transcendental Meditationalists have their mantras. Because you repeat these repetitive predetermined prayers enough and they lose their meaning. So these words that have no rational meaning are falling through your mind. And what happens? The analytic flow stops. You prolong the moment of no voice in your head, and it induces a kind of spiritual high. The religions give this to you as a way to live, a way to get in touch with God.

Well, the artist has got to find a way to do something similar, although it cannot be—and this is harder for you— through repetitive, predetermined bits of text. Nevertheless, the only way to create a work of literary art is to stop that voice. Your total attention needs to be on the sensual flow of experience from the unconscious.

One of the ways of understanding your unconscious is by realizing that in order to get into it you have to actually stop that garbagey analytical reflex voice in your head and induce a kind of trance state. Religious trances are quite common. Well, there's a trance state also that the artist must induce in herself in order to create a work of art. You have to let go of that comforting, distancing voice, you have to then descend into that deep dream space of yours, and that will result in a kind of superconcentration.

Psychologists call it the "flow state," being in the flow. Athletes call it being "in the zone."

The athlete's zone and the artist's creative trance have a great deal in common. When I was teaching in Louisiana, a friend of mine was assistant athletic director at LSU. His name was Greg LeFleur, and he was once an excellent tight end for the then St. Louis Cardinals NFL football team. Greg and I at some point came to understand that what he did and what I do have this need for a trancelike state in common.

How did Greg take off at full speed, run twenty-five, thirty yards down the field while behind him his quarterback— I think it was Jim Hart—launched this odd-shaped object into the air—and Greg is running full tilt down the field and two linebackers are converging on him to crush the life out of his body, and Greg glances over his shoulder and throws his body out, extends his hands, and this object settles gently under his fingertips and he holds it even as he falls to the ground and the linebackers fall on top of him. How did he do that?

Well, I tell you how you don't do it and that's by thinking about it. Any athlete will tell you. Jackie Stewart, the great race car driver, said in his autobiography that when you drive a car really fast and really well, you don't have a sensation of speed at all; things slow down around you, you can count the bricks on the wall at the next turn. Baseball players, when they are batting and in a streak, say they can count the stitches on the ball. They are in the zone, and that means they are not thinking at all. They call it *muscle memory*. But for you, it's not muscle memory; it's dream space, it's sense memory. It is *not* literal memory, the thing that's made you good at school.

If the athlete begins to send the process into his head, he goes into a slump. He misses the basket, he misses that turn. Lights out. He drops the ball. I think, by the way, that's why athletes are so superstitious. Because if you believe that your current batting streak depends on wearing a pair of dirty socks, you're less likely to think it has to do with your technique. If it's technique, you think about it. If it's your socks, it's not rational. What superstitions do for the athlete is to irrationalize. And that's what you have to do as a writer; you have to irrationalize yourself somehow.

Now, there's one big difference between the athlete's zone and the artist's zone. And this is another way of explaining the challenge of Kurosawa's observation. Let's look at Michael Jordan in his later prime—let's say his last season with the Bulls, when they once again won the world championship. When Michael received a pass at the top of the key in full flight and he left the ground, he defied gravity, floated through the air, let that ball roll off his fingertips and into the basket. Tongue unconsciously extended. When he did that, he had to be in the zone. He could not be thinking about what he was doing. But to make his zone exactly analogous to the art zone, you have to add this: every time he shoots, in order to make a basket Michael Jordan would have to confront, without flinching, the moment when his father's chest was blown apart by the shotgun held by his kidnapper. You know that happened in Michael Jordan's life. Well, Michael would have to confront that in order to make a basket every time. Without flinching. Now his zone is equal to the artist's zone. And now you understand the challenge of being an artist.

2

THE ZONE

"All good novelists have bad memories."
—Graham Greene

The great British novelist Graham Greene said that all good novelists have bad memories. What you remember comes out as journalism. What you forget goes into the compost of the imagination. I want you to remember that Graham Greene quotation—though in fact it's a paraphrase because I can't remember the quote—because in a compost heap, things decompose. Your past is full of stories that have been composed in a certain way; that's what memories are. But only when they decompose are you able to recompose them into new works of art.

You can see where I'm going. Greene's compost of the imagination is the same as the dreamspace, the white-hot center of the unconscious. The point he's making is that not only is your mind the enemy, not only is your will, your rational thinking, your analytic thinking the enemy, but your literal memories are also the enemy. How many times have you heard a short story criticized and heard the author say,

That's the way it happened. It can't be unreal because it happened that way.

But a work of art is an organic thing. Every detail must organically resonate with every other detail. If you have an intransigent literal memory—and intransigent is what literal memories are—it sits in the middle of the organic object; it destroys everything around it. Everything in a work must remain malleable, everything must remain negotiable. You need to understand that working from your literal memory will keep you out of your unconscious, out of the zone you must enter.

I'm going to give you some practical suggestions on how to get into your zone or dreamspace. The first of those suggestions is, in fact, more than merely practical; it is rooted in the psychology of creation. Once you are engaged in writing a piece of fiction from your unconscious, it is crucial that you write every day, because the nature of this place where you go is such that it's very difficult to find your way in. It's pure torture. But even though it's terrible getting in, once you're in, if you keep going back every day, though it's still always daunting and difficult and scary, it's not nearly so much so. You may find—this is dangerous, but you may find—that you can take a day off every six or seven days. When you do, you'll be grumpy and out of sorts and things will be uncomfortable, but after a day you can go back in. But you take two days off and you're on very thin ice. If you let three or four days go by it's as if you've never written a word in your entire life. That doorway closes and seals itself up; you don't even know what part of the wall that door's in anymore. I don't care how much you've written in your life; those defenses are strong and they won't let you go there.

You may not be ready to write yet, but when you're in a project you must write every day. You cannot write just on weekends. You cannot write this week and not next; you can't wait for the summer to write. You can't skip the summer and wait till the fall. You have to write every day. You cannot do it any other way. Have I said this strongly enough?

There are no excuses not to write. At some point in my life, for various personal reasons, the only opportunity I had to write was on the Long Island Rail Road as I commuted from my home in Long Island to a job as editor-in-chief of a business newspaper in Manhattan. This was before laptop computers. I wrote every word of my first four published novels on my lap, on legal pads, by hand, on the Long Island Rail Road, where the air-conditioning never worked in the summer, and the heat never worked in the winter, and it was always jam-packed, and people were flapping their papers and yakking and killing each other over the wrong bridge bid three seats up in front of me.

But eventually a thing kicked in that psychologists used to call *functional fixedness*. That is, if you have a certain place and certain objects that you associate only with a certain task, eventually the associational values build up in such a way that when you go to that place and engage those objects, you are instantly completely focused on that task. So getting over the hump of distraction with those railroad trips eventually became an asset, because writing was all I ever did on the train; I did nothing else. And I began to write well. I wrote my first four published novels on that train.

So here's one of those practical suggestions for getting into the zone. Find a place and some objects that you go to and engage only when you're writing fiction. If you have only one space and one computer that you must use for all written things, then change the type font you use for your fiction or the color of your screen.

By the way, I finally got a teaching job that took me off the train. I got my Ph.D. at the "University of Knopf"—that is, I accumulated enough publishing credits to get a university teaching job—and I went to McNeese State University in Lake Charles, Louisiana. I was halfway through my fifth novel—it was already under contract to Knopf and my editor loved the first half and I did too—and I had to stop writing to drive my furniture across the country in a U-Haul, finish buying a house, and move in. I stopped writing for eight weeks. And when I returned to the novel, though I knew those characters as well as any real person I've ever known, and though I knew what was going to happen next in the plot, it was utter agony to return to the work. It took eight weeks of daily torture to write another sentence—because I'd stopped writing every day. Also, if you develop functional fixedness to help you, you can't then let it be an excuse not to write. If you are away from the conditions you've established, you must still write every day. For a while I blamed my not writing on the fact that the room wasn't moving. I thought I was going to have to buy a little motor and stick it on my chair to jiggle it. Maybe buy choo-choo sounds for my record player. But of course the real problem was the broken link to my unconscious caused by putting the work aside for a time.

Another practical way to facilitate your entry into your writing zone is to turn yourself into a morning person. If you arrange your life so that you can spend two hours writing—or an hour, given the exigencies of some working lives, but ideally a couple of hours—you make that time sacrosanct at the beginning of the day. If you need coffee, you put your coffee on a timer, you roll out of bed, you grab that cup of coffee, and you are at your computer keyboard only moments from a literal dreamspace.

Finding a way to clear your sensibility of abstract uses of language is important to get into the trance. The problem is that we naturally use language in so many nonsensual ways all through the day. I find it helpful, then, to buffer those hours in which you necessarily use language in those analytical ways from the hours in which you dive into your unconscious and seek language in quite another way. One obvious way to do that is to put your night's sleep in between. You go into your writing space straight from another dream state and go to language before you've had a chance for all those other uses of language to intrude on you. So after you wake up, don't read the newspaper, don't watch CNN; if you have to pee don't pick up the back issue of *The New Yorker* in the basket nearby. You go to your fiction writing without letting *any* conceptual language into your head.

I almost always write to music, and that might be helpful to some of you. I've almost never written any fiction without carefully chosen music, usually classical or jazz, almost always without words—I've been known to write to Puccini, though if I understood Italian I probably couldn't. But whatever helps you go into your trance state—whether quiet is right or music helps—in any case, you do need to be visiting your unconscious every day.

The crucial awareness you must keep is this: do not will the work. Do not write until it's coming from your unconscious. If you have the itch to write before inspiration has visited you, spend that time meditating in your unconscious. That said, there is a type of journaling that I could recommend, especially at this stage of your development. Most journaling is counterproductive. Most journals are repositories of great swatches of abstraction and generalization and self-analysis and interpretation and all that bad stuff. Don't do that. But here's a certain kind of journal that might be useful to you: at the end of the day or beginning of the next day, return to some event of the day that evoked an *emotion* in you. Record that event in the journal. But do this only—*only*—moment to moment through the senses. Absolutely never name an emotion; never start explaining or analyzing or interpreting an emotion. Record only through those five ways I mentioned that we feel emotions—signals inside the body, signals outside the body, flashes of the past, flashes of the future, sensual selectivity—which are therefore the best ways to express emotions. Such a journal entry will read like a passage in a novel, like the most intense moment-to-moment scene in a novel. And that's all that will be there. Fully developed in the moment.

If you write in your journal every day in this way, and if you spend forty-five minutes or an hour at it, it will be so intensive that you might not get through the whole incident.

That's fine. Just break it off, don't try to summarize or bring it to the end. Next day you might pick it up again. Or not. Go for some other piece of another emotional event. And don't rely so heavily on the sense reactions within your body that when you read this fifteen years from now all you get is "palpitating heart" and "sweating palms" and "blurry vision," which could be reactions to anything. This should be rendered as if it were a scene, with all the external and internal events.

After you've got a couple of weeks' worth of these entries, the entry of two weeks ago will have had a chance to cool off. From then on, each day's journaling should have two parts to it. First, write a new entry. Then, when you've finished, go back and read the journal entry of two weeks ago, and with a marker pen slash through all the examples of abstraction, generalization, summary, analysis, and interpretation you see in the text, leaving only moment-to-moment sense-based events and impressions. No matter how much you intended to write "in the moment," I promise you those old habits will have come back, but the hope is that, over the course of time, the red marks will diminish.

Even if you're doing a sense-based journal, you're going to have serious trouble between your creative projects. This is when you'll understand why the need to write every day runs so deep. When I've finished a work, and some time passes, and I'm working up to something new, I feel that I am utterly wasting my life. I do trivial, ghastly, quotidian stuff; I hate myself; I complain about myself to my wife, and that hatred daily increases. Finally she says to me, "Honey, it's OK, you've now reached total self-loathing; you're about to start writing." She's

always right. Soon thereafter, the door opens up to my unconscious, to my new work, and I leap in. And then I write every
day and I am scared every day and I am happy every day.

A word about writer's block here. I think writer's block
probably suggests that you have an artist's instinct. Bad writers never get blocked. Writers who write from their heads and
are comfortable doing that—they always have some garbage
to put down. I talked last week about the flow of metathink-
ing, metaspeaking your mind. That stuff's always there and it's
easy to put it on the page. I think most writers who get blocked
do so because some important part of them knows that they've
got to get to the unconscious. But they're not getting there;
they're thinking too much, so there's nothing there. Except
it's not quite nothing—you sit there thinking, fussing, and
worrying: "Gee, I'm not writing," "I've got to write now and
I'm not writing," "Oh my God, I'm not writing," "If I want to
be a writer I've got to write and I'm not writing." I think
writer's block of that sort is the most common kind among
writers who have any talent.

Writer's block is very similar to insomnia. What happens
in insomnia? You lie down, intending to go into your dreamspace, literally; into the depths of your unconscious, where you
totally lose touch with the outer world. That's what sleep is. But
you can't do it. Why? Because you can't turn your mind off. You
lie there thinking about things. And if there are images, it's only
because you're carefully controlling them. You sometimes have
a kind of daydream going on, but you're in charge of it. You're
making it happen, and you get upset about this and you think
about that and you argue about this, and all the time there's

this "Gee, I still am not sleeping, am I?" and, "OK, there's my mother. Gee, I'm thinking about her. I don't want to think about my mother, she makes me mad. What would I say to her if she called right now? I'd tell her . . ." That's what's going on in your head, right?

What happens when you finally do fall asleep? Suddenly an image comes out of nowhere: a rainy street, a street lamp, a dog barking. Whoa, where did that come from? Nowhere. And at the moment that image comes, if you ask, "Well, where *did* that come from?"—it's gone; nothing will follow and you've got thirty-five more minutes of being awake.

Those of you who *don't* have trouble with insomnia, think about how you go to sleep. You lie down and all that garbage just turns off. Suddenly an image comes, and another, and boy, then you're gone. And that's how you write.

It's a funny state. It's not as if you're falling asleep at your computer, but neither are you brainstorming. You're *dreamstorming*, inviting the images of moment-to-moment experience through your unconscious. It's very much like an intensive daydream, but a daydream that you are and are not controlling. You let it go, but it's coming through language that you're putting on a screen, so there is some intervention on your part, and yet the essence of it—that rainy street and that dog barking and the lamplight—are nothing you're going after consciously. The state of communion with your unconscious—the zone I'm trying to describe—is absolutely essential, *absolutely essential* to writing well in this art form.

Where does language come into this very-hard-to-describe, mystical sort of place—what I'm calling your unconscious—

when you create a work of art? When I talk about the place of language in this process, it's another way to speak of voice. *Voice is the embodiment in language of the contents of your unconscious.* When you turn off that flow of garbage in your head, you're turning off certain kinds of words—you're turning off abstract and analytical metawords. What then takes their place is a very strong presence of language, but it's almost misleading to call it language because language is so often used in those ways that mean analysis, abstraction. That's why I say voice. The presence of words—which you quickly capture and string together and massage—is intimately bound up with that sensual imagery in your unconscious, which makes up your voice and the voices of your characters.

The line-to-line words come from your unconscious and so does the very form in which you write. You do not know whether you're a novelist or a short story writer. You don't choose ahead of time to be a novelist and then look around in yourself and figure out what novels you've got there. You have a vision of the world and that vision has a natural form; you don't know what will turn out to be the natural form of your vision. You've probably had the experience of writing a short story that just kind of takes off. It's not a very good story, because what you're seeing really wants to be a novel. Or you sit down trying to write a novel and you poop out at about page 40. That happens because you are forcing your vision into a predetermined medium, and that's not the way it should work.

The distinction between the vision that becomes a novel and the vision that becomes a short story is pretty much like this (I'm going to describe these differences metaphorically; I am not advocating a consciousness of your audience): the short story will have you say to the reader, "Look, I don't have much time. So sit down, let me tell you about a moment in this character's life when something took a turn, or something intensified in some significant way." The short story will have, oftentimes, a brief sequence of causally linked events, but ultimately it turns *on the moment*.

The novel is going to be saying to your reader, "Look, this is going to take some time. Let's go for a long walk, and I want to tell you about all these things that happened in the life of this character in my unconscious; all these things that happened to him, which somehow fit together, are somehow causally linked." In a novel, there will be many revealing moments but ultimately the focus of a novel is on that—I won't call it a chain, because that argues for a certain kind of linear structure, but—that certain configuration of causally linked events. That's the focus of a novel.

Oftentimes I've found that my novels come out of the wedding of two separate visions that seemed to be two different novels, two books that really weren't working and seemed quite different from each other. (I've got a number of potential novels and stories running around in my unconscious at any given meditative moment.)

Let me go back to one of those really god-awful novels that never saw the light of day, my first Vietnam-based novel, called *What Lies Near*. It was about a guy in military intelligence who visits the holding cell in an interrogation camp for suspected Viet Cong. He goes into a cell vacated by a prisoner who's been tortured and taken somewhere else, and he finds a piece of graffiti written on the wall. The novel I wrote was just straight out of literal memory stuff. As a military intelligence agent, I had gone to an interrogation center run by the ARVNs—the Army of the Republic of Vietnam, which is South Vietnamese—and there was a cell where they kept the Viet Cong prisoners while they tortured them—horribly, as the South Vietnamese often did. I went in the cell and—these are the tropics; it was a hundred degrees and 95 percent humidity outside this windowless space about six feet square, which had an iron door with a little plate kept shut and a stone ledge for sleeping and a hole in the floor—I stepped in and instantly broke into a heavy sweat from the closeness of the air and the foul smells from the hole in the floor, and the walls were stained with lichen, and I was ready to turn and flee.

But—I don't know what made me think of this—I wondered about graffiti. Was there some trace of the people left behind? I looked at the walls, and there were obviously some places that had been scratched—the scratchings then obliterated by the caretakers of the place. Very carefully monitored. There was nothing else to see, and I was about to leave when I noticed a little wooden stand against one wall. I thought, well, if somebody wanted to put some graffiti where it would survive scrutiny, he'd put it behind that. So I pulled that stand away from the wall and suddenly heard the frantic rustle of brittle little feet, and dozens of three-inch cockroaches scattered from behind this thing—just that last turn of the horror of the place: these people are kept in darkness with roaches crawling all over, waiting to be tortured—and, sure enough, there was a piece of graffiti scratched into the wall behind the wooden stand.

It read, "*Vệ siuh là khoẻ,*" which means, "Hygiene is healthful."

Suddenly I was in the presence of this remarkable mind. To have that kind of irony, that kind of detachment!

Well, I wrote the terrible novel called *What Lies Near,* in which the agent finds this graffiti and then spends the rest of the novel trying to track down the guy who wrote it. I myself didn't try to track him down; the novel was driven by what had happened there, in that cell, and I was just sort of tunnel-visioned onto it. It was slavish to what really happened, and that was not enough to sustain a novel. It was not a novel.

In 1983, ten years after the failure of *What Lies Near,* I had found my way into my unconscious and just published *Countrymen of Bones.* I began my fourth novel and moved from the fine but rather obscure independent company, Horizon Press, to Knopf. In those ten years, I'd had another notion for a novel—let's face it, it was an *idea*; that's why it was not going anywhere—based on the fact that my son had been born and looked just like me—a little externalization of self. I wrote an awful short story about it—but one that led me to consider how American army men went to Vietnam for a year: you drop into war, and they pluck you out again. There were legions of Vietnamese women in the gray area between prostitute and aspiring girlfriend, and they didn't understand birth control or didn't give a damn, so there were a lot of children born of fleeting connections—"children of the dust." There were men who lived for thirty years in America not knowing that they had a child, now an adult somewhere in the world. They would go to their graves probably not giving it a thought, and certainly not knowing that they had a part of themselves in the world. Still, that's not enough for a novel. And it was a bad short story.

Actually twelve years had passed since I was in Vietnam—and now two separate things that had gotten me to meditate there, the prisoner and the child, suddenly came together in my unconscious. Only when those things converged was there the fullness of a novel. *On Distant Ground* is about an army intelligence captain being tried in a court martial for having tracked down and set free a Viet Cong prisoner—prompted to do so by seeing graffiti written on a wall. His yearning is for a connection with the other, and this yearning has been intensified by a son who looks just like him, though he is a man of inherent emotional distance and aloofness toward everyone around him including his wife. During the trial he becomes obsessed with the memory of a Vietnamese woman who mysteriously broke off their affair, and he wonders if he may be one of those people unknowingly with a child in Vietnam. He goes back—he's on bail—to Saigon. The city falls while he's there, and he's trapped in Communist Vietnam, looking for a child who may not exist.

To choose the novel or short story form without it being driven by a vision from your unconscious is a big mistake. If you are to propel your work without some willed preconception, then nothing must be preconceived, including the form, the content, and especially memories of the events of your life that produced the inspiration. You will get legitimate artistic inspiration from your unconscious, and often part of you will know where it came from. But then you have to resist going back, finding all the old notes, and working out what really happened in the past.

Be alert to the fact that you must achieve a trancelike state in order to write from your unconscious. You'll also have to know what to look for in the stuff that's coming off of the tips of your fingers. You can see the bad stuff going up on the screen; you know where it's coming from. You don't just let yourself get away with it.

And, of course, writing is also rewriting. I need to say a final word now on the question of editing and rewriting: you might say to yourself, OK, that's fine, all that white-hot-center stuff spilling out in the composition, but when I go back to edit and revise, how do the dreams fit in there? Or do they?

They absolutely do. What you need to do now is to think of yourself as a reader encountering a strange work. You've got to understand your own memory and figure out what it takes for you to forget what you have written, sufficiently that you can revisit it as reader. That's the key to editing yourself. This is where having a bad memory will serve you well. If you re-read your work without having forgotten it, you'll be analyzing your own work in all those lit-crit ways. I'm lucky. I literally forget my sentences after I've written them. I will write a sentence; I'll write another; I'll go back and read the previous sentence, and I won't know where the hell it came from.

I'll have more to say about reading a little later, but the essence is this: the primary and only necessary way of experiencing a work of literary art is not by "understanding" it in analytical terms; it is by *thrumming* to the work of art. Like the string of a stringed instrument you vibrate inside, a harmonic is set up. So to edit your work, you go back and thrum to it. And you go *thrum, thrum, thrum, twang!* And when you go *twang!* as a reader, mark that passage. And you thrum on and twang on and thrum and twang and thrum and twang. Then you go back to the twangs and instead of looking at the twangy spots and analyzing them in lit-crit ways, instead of consciously and wilfully applying what you understand with your mind about craft and techniques, you *redream* those passages.

Rewriting is redreaming. Rewriting is redreaming till it all thrums.

Let me return to Graham Greene. The compost heap of the novelist, the repository that exists apart from literal memory, apart from the conscious mind, is mostly made up of direct, sensual life experience. But it is also the proper place for all the fiction craft and technique that you properly and necessarily consciously learned. It is also the proper place for all the wonderful fiction you've read. All of these things must first be forgotten—at least while you are in your creative trance—before they can be authentically engaged in the creation of a work of art.

3

YEARNING

"There is no theory. You have merely to listen."
—*Claude Debussy*

What I'm going to talk about tonight is an essential of fiction as an art form—as essential as color is to painting and movement is to dance and sound is to music.

I would say that of the three fundamentals of fiction, there are two that aspiring writers never miss: first, that fiction is about human beings; second, that it's about human emotion. Even when fiction writers are writing from their heads, abstracting and analyzing, they're mostly analyzing emotions; so even if they're not getting at the essence of emotion, they're trying to.

But the third element, which is missing from virtually every student manuscript I've seen, has to do with the phenomenon of desire.

Fiction is a temporal art form. Fiction exists in time. Poems by contrast are very condensed objects, virtually exempt from time. A poem may capture a fleeting momentary impulse; and the length of a line is usually a part of its essential form, so the poem is also an object on the page. But as soon as you let the line run on and you turn the page, you are *upon a time*, inevitably. And, as any Buddhist will tell you, you cannot exist as a human being on this planet for thirty seconds without desiring something.

My favorite word in this regard—a word you will hear often when we discuss your manuscripts—is *yearning*. We yearn. We are the yearning creatures of this planet. There are superficial yearnings, and there are truly deep ones always pulsing beneath, but every second we yearn for *something*. And fiction, inescapably, is the art form of human yearning.

Yearning is *always* part of fictional character. In fact, one way to understand plot is that it represents the *dynamics of desire*. It's the dynamics of desire that is at the heart of narrative and plot.

Those failed manuscripts of students and aspiring writers—many of them showing a lot of talent—contained characters with problems, attitudes, opinions, sensibility, voice, personality—all of those things, and often a wonderfully evoked milieu to boot. But none of those things automatically carries with it yearning. The dynamics of desire can be utterly missing from a story that is rich with all of those things.

James Joyce appropriated from the Catholic church the term *epiphany*. An epiphany literally means "a shining forth." He brought that concept to bear on the moment in a work of art when something shines forth in its essence. That, he said, is the epiphany in a story or novel.

What I would suggest is that there are two epiphanies in any good work of fiction. Joyce's is the second, the one often called the climax or crisis of a story. The first epiphany comes very near the beginning, where the sensual details accumulate around a moment in which the deepest yearning of the main character shines forth. The reader responds in a deep visceral way to that first epiphany—and that's the epiphany missing from virtually every student manuscript I've read.

It is an element also, of course, missing from much published fiction. Various stories you read may leave you a little cold, distanced—you may admire, maybe you have a kind of "smart" reaction—but nothing resonates in the marrow of your bones, and the reason is that the character's yearning is not manifest.

This lack is interesting, because writers who aspire to a different kind of fiction—entertainment fiction, let's call it, genre fiction—have never forgotten this necessity of the character's yearning. Maybe that's why they're selling books and we're not—because you cannot find a book on the bestseller list without a central character who clearly wants something, is driving for something, has a clear objective: *I want to solve the crime. I want to kill the monster. I want to go to bed with that woman or that man. I want to win the war.* You name the genre. Every story has a character full of desire.

The difference between the desires expressed in entertainment fiction and literary fiction is only a difference of level. Instead of: *I want a man, a woman, wealth, power,* or *to solve a mystery* or *to drive a stake through a vampire's heart,* a literary desire is on the order of: *I yearn for self, I yearn for an identity, I yearn for a place in the universe, I yearn to connect to the other*. But that there must be yearning the genre writers never forget. We do.

Desire is the driving force behind plot. The character yearns, the character does something in pursuit of that yearning, and some force or other will block the attempt to fulfill that yearning. The character will respond to the force in some way, go round or through or over or under it, and continue the pursuit. This dynamic beneath the story is plot: the attempt to fulfill the yearning and the world's attempt to thwart that.

Most of the time, good fiction comes out of an inspiration that includes an intuition of yearning. In your unconscious, in your dreamspace, a character presents herself to you. She is a product of your own deepest white-hot center, but she is an *other*. When she presents herself, there will probably be a place involved, or an external circumstance, perhaps even a moment in our history—a crash, a war, the death of a mother —not your mother, understand, but the death of this character's mother. There will probably be an event that comes to you somehow, which summons her up. This character is summoned into your unconscious. You recognize her there, those luminous events and places surround her; but however vivid she seems to you, you may not yet be ready to write her story if the yearning is not there. For me, the thing that triggers the moment in my unconscious when a character is ready to speak or be spoken of, ready to be a story, is a flash of intuition about that character's yearning. *What is it at her deepest level that she yearns for?*

Until a character with yearning has emerged from your unconscious, I don't encourage you to write. Again, I empha-

size intuition. It's not that you come to some intellectual understanding. It's an intuition of her wanting, a sense of her
desiring. And then you're ready to write.

But perhaps you have a character pressing himself upon
you and you don't feel that intuitive connection to his yearning. Try to wait for it. But if it's just not coming, you can begin
to write in the way you have done in most of your manuscripts
so far—moving around in the problems of the character, trying on the voice of a narrator, exploring the character's attitudes and opinions and reactions. However, it is crucial you
understand that this isn't the work of art you've commenced
to create. It is a kind of line-to-line rumination. A working
exercise. You must realize that all you're doing here is keeping your eyes and ears open for that whiff of true, dynamic
yearning in your character. At the moment you get that whiff,
you stop writing this thing and put it away and never look at
it again. You'll hear these words again from me in a later context. It's equally important here. Once you have that link to
your character's yearning, only then does the real work of literary fiction begin.

So then you need to reenter your character's world afresh
and dream your way into whatever it is that might upset the
equilibrium of that world. You will seek what is called the "inciting incident." Things are in balance in the world of this
character, and then the equilibrium is upset by the inciting
incident. This does not necessarily have to occur within the
story; it often doesn't. But somehow the world of the character becomes unbalanced, and this challenges whatever it is the
character deeply yearns for. And this is how things begin.

Following the "inciting incident" is the "point of attack"—these terms are commonly used in connection with plot, but I think it's important to remind you about them in regard to yearning. Both can occur at the same moment, but because the inciting incident may well have happened prior to the beginning of the story, there may equally be a separate point of attack. To use a dramatic analogy: in *Hamlet*, the inciting incident is the murder of Hamlet's father, which has occurred well before the rising of the curtain. The point of attack is the appearance of the father's ghost to Hamlet.

Point of attack, which introduces the conflict—the particular manifestation of a character's yearning—is an important notion because when you write a story you need to make sure that something is at stake. It doesn't need to be an external thing; it must have inner magnitude, though. Your character's yearning is deep and important; you need to treat it with respect.

Conflict can be internal or external. An external conflict pits the character against the natural world, or society, or other characters. The internal conflict exists between or among various aspects of the character's own self. I think it's rare that a literary work touches the deepest realms of human experience without presenting some sort of internal conflict. Often in the most exciting literary works, an internal conflict runs parallel to, or resonates through, some larger conflict in the external world. That interaction between the inner and the outer is a unique provenance of narrative. No other art form can really grasp the interaction between the external world and the internal world as fiction can.

Let's deal again for a moment with the distinction between literature and nonliterature. I talked about what it
means to be an artist, why people become artists, what the
sensibility of an artist is, where you have to look in yourself to
be an artist; and I have even, in terms of yearning, com-
plimented our nonartist writer colleagues. But I think it's
important to make a couple of distinctions regarding attention to the moment-by-moment sensual flow of experience,
which I claim as necessary to art in fiction.

Nonart, genre writing, entertainment writing, is typi-
cally filled with abstraction, generalization, summary, analysis, and interpretation. I ran across a book a few months ago
in a Borders somewhere, called *The Romance Writer's Phrase
Book,* in which you could look up an emotion and find fifty
punchy phrases to describe it. Passion, for instance: "Her
heart beat wild with passion." I pulled out that example because it's somewhat deceptive. There does seem to be a sense
impression there. We talked about the five ways we can feel
emotions through our senses; one of them is a sensual reaction within your body. Isn't the wildly beating heart such a
thing?

Yes, strictly speaking, it is. We had a faculty meeting
today in the commons room on the ground floor of this building, and when I came out there was a great crowd around the
elevator, and I was with Rip Lhamon, who's in seriously good
shape. He said, "Too many people, let's walk." Not wanting
to seem a wimp, I said, "Sure," and we walked up five floors.
My heart was beating wildly by the end of this climb. It was
not from passion.

That particular internal sense impression is so easy, so widely applicable, as to have the impact of an abstraction. "My heart was beating wildly"; we don't know what that's all about. Well, "with passion." Now, *passion* is an abstraction—you know, you're feeling "passion"; you have an intellectual response to that.

Let's go back to the romance novel example—believe me, men have their literary equivalents—and say that within a half-mile radius of this room tonight, there is a woman sitting in her study or in her kitchen, and her own heart is beating wildly in empathy. She is weeping, she is growing ardent— that's an abstraction, but that's what we're talking right now— over such sentences as "Her heart beat wild with passion." Does that not prove that this is literature? How is that not art if it can induce that kind of reaction in a reader?

It is not art, because her emotional response is a result of her filling in the blanks left by that abstraction. The direct, visceral response to the text results from her filling in from her own fantasies, her own past, and her own aspirations. Abstract, summarizing, generalizing, and analytic language will induce the reader to fill in the blanks and thereby distance her from the work and the characters. The moment-to-moment, fresh, organically connected sense impressions of the work of art will draw the reader into it. In the emotional reaction to a work of art, you do not fill in from yourself; you leave yourself. You enter into the character and into the character's sensibility and psychology and spirit and world. It's the difference between masturbation and making love. The former is a self-referential experience; you have, on the surface, a similar response, but it's a closed loop. In making love, you leave yourself and enter into the other; that is the experience between two people who are connecting in deeper ways. And that's the experience of literature.

I am talking here about the reader's experience, but we understand that what the writer puts on the page produces that experience. This is another important difference between the creation of a fictional work of art and a work of entertainment. The evidence is in the text. Nonartists—and I would include not only entertainment writers, by the way, but didactic writers as well; not only Stephen King but, let's say, Jean-Paul Sartre as a novelist—before they write a single word, the nonartists know exactly the effect they wish to have on their readers, whether emotional or intellectual. Stephen King wants to scare the hell out of you. Jean-Paul Sartre wants, well, to scare the hell out of you, but also to convince you of the cosmic verities inherent in the existentialist worldview. These writers know these effects ahead of time and so they construct an object to produce them.

But the artist *does not know*. She doesn't know what she knows about the world until she creates the object. For the artist, the writing of a work of art is as much an act of exploration as it is expression, an exploration of images, of moment-to-moment sensual experience. And this exploration comes from the nature of art and the nature of the artistic process as I've been trying to describe it to you.

Since I have been insisting on the dangers of abstraction, I'm going to offer you a potentially very dangerous paradox. I'm going to give you a loaded gun and tell you to stick it into your mouth. You hear me talking about the antiartistic modes of discourse: generalization, interpretation, and so forth. If you read a fairy tale it's always flat and disappointing and full of summary, yet all of us have had intense, memorable experiences of them. A fairy tale is not really meant to be read on the page, and your memory of that kind of story originates, let's say—let's not talk about Florida, but up north—on a cold winter night, fresh out of a hot bath, snuggled into the covers—got them up to your ears—the wind is blowing outside you can hear it in the eaves of the house—your mother is sitting at your elbow, the lamp is low, and she's reading this fairy tale to you, and the voice goes up and down. Your toes are warm now and it's a ravishing experience. It's those other elements that make for the moment-to-moment sensual experience of that kind of storytelling.

A similar experience can potentially occur in a work of literary art, because the narrator sits in your sensibility as a character. The voice of that character can offer the reader a sensual moment-to-moment experience. For a later session you all will have read my short story "Open Arms" [see appendix]. In the first sentence, the narrator says, "I have no hatred in me." Well, *hatred* is an abstraction, and it's a bit of an analysis. But the next sentence is "I'm almost certain of that." With that "almost" we have a context in which we hear something different from what he's saying. Dramatic irony is now at work. We have a place to stand that allows us to interpret differently from the way he interprets. His abstraction doesn't engage our minds; it engages us in the response to his personality, which is a sensual response.

You will find many voices, even in extended passages, that use some abstraction or analysis in literary fiction, but you will never find those modes of discourse used for surface effects or surface information. They have to do with the sensual presence of voice. This is especially true of first person narrators, but each third person voice also is absolutely distinctive. All writing, in fact, has a narrative persona—your cereal box this morning had a personality. All writing has within it a persona identifiable by diction, vocabulary, syntax. You don't analyze it. You respond to it directly.

You understand why this is a dangerous notion for you, when you're still trying to find your way into your unconscious and trying not to avert your eyes? The little voice that has failed to get you to cut your nails instead of writing, or clean the toilet instead of writing, or read a good book instead of writing—that little voice is going to seize on this paradox and say, "Oh well, my character can explain that; it's just his character." Very dangerous.

I want now to give you some examples from literature of this slippery, evasive, most important thing called yearning. I'm going to read four passages from four diverse works by four wonderful writers and then look at them in terms of yearning.

The first piece is the opening of Janet Burroway's novel, *Cutting Stone*, a novel set back early in the twentieth century. Eleanor, our point-of-view character, and her husband, Laurel, are on a train heading west. He has tuberculosis. They're going to Arizona for his health; he's taken a job there as a bank manager. Notice that the yearning is not addressed here explicitly, but the first epiphany happens very early.

Outside the club car window, flat desert nothing as far as the eye could see; endless stubble in level light. They were still two days short of Arizona. Eleanor sipped an early aperitif, perspiring jagged rings on the armholes of her pongee suit. Laurel was skimming a *Commerce Chronicle*, occasionally coughing a discreet, dry cough. He had taken off his jacket, self-deprecating, murmuring, "When in Rome . . . ," and in pin-striped vest and four-in-hand he looked crisp, compact.

Under the rhythmic chug of the train ran a thinner sound, a continuous screech of metal on metal that put Eleanor in mind of rending silk. She felt this image through her abdomen as if the track were a single tear all the way back to Maryland. A copy of *House Beautiful* lay in her lap, and she read, "No nation has studied homebuilding so persistently and long as the English, and consequently none has arrived at anything like such general excellence."

This sentence had nothing to do with her and could not logically be met with grief. But the raw lot of her unbuilt house rose in her mind, overgrown with lush creeper, a stand of oak. She had spent the better part of a year imagining, then sketching, a façade in that little Baltimore wilderness, and a layout she knew so well that she could walk it out on the ground.

She was losing everything. Everything in memory and all that never was to be; and things the more poignant because she hadn't noticed that she cared for them. The wood planes in Daddy's warehouse, her hand patting along the shelf as she told over their names by heart: *plow, bull nose, dado, beading, rabbet, slitting.* Who ever would have thought she'd grieve for the planes?

"Outside the club car window, flat desert nothing as far as the eye can see; endless stubble in level light." This is our first image. We have not yet placed the point of view, although we will shortly see that this is Eleanor's perception and see the landscape as revealing character. What's missing there? First of all, there's no home, no house, there's no place to live here, and—interestingly—there's no verb. Very quickly, the yearning for a place in the world becomes clear. In a world where there is no place, there is no life, and so the very part of speech which signifies life and movement is missing from the first image in the book. A pseudosentence—even, ironically, a semicolon, as though there were sentences on either side, but it's grammatical nonsense—displays the fact that there's no verb, no life. I talked to you about the organic nature of art, everything echoing everything else. This is a wonderful example of that.

"They were still two days short of Arizona. Eleanor sipped an early aperitif, perspiring jagged rings on the armholes of her pongee suit." A silk suit, pongee silk. And what we now see is this arid place, and a woman out of place, displaced, but in the reflexes of a life that is about to change. Sipping "an aperitif." I dare say the word had never been spoken in Arizona in 1914. Laurel "skimming a *Commerce Chronicle*"—again, it's as if they were sitting in their parlor, whereas in fact they're being carried far away from the life of their past. And Eleanor is

conscious of that. We're in her point of view, so we understand that she's aware of the jagged rings of sweat. Laurel's first
comment is "When in Rome"—a facile patrician use of a
cliché, just because he's taking off his coat. He's still dressed
in his pinstriped vest and four-in-hand!

We hear the train running, and the very movement of
the thing carrying her away suggests—what?—the rending of
silk. Silk already represents the life that she's lived, and it's
being rent apart, and then she's all the way back to Maryland.
It's *House Beautiful!* she reads, talking of homebuilding in
England and, meanwhile, the desert is all around them. We
find that she has an unbuilt house—and this is where the
epiphany of yearning is strongest. Because her grief is not just
for aperitifs and silk dresses. In fact her potential is separate
from her privilege—and where is that potential found? In the
intense memory of something very concrete, very sensual, very
specific: her father's wood planes. And then comes that wonderful verb, her hand *patting* along the shelf, touching these
planes and knowing the rich, various names of them. As we
see that potential for something of the hands, of building something new, we see that potential *in her*. She grieves not for her
parlor and her silk dresses, but for the planes—and that's where
the yearning comes through clearest. If you combine that
moment with the devastating desert image in the beginning,
her yearning suggests, ironically, her potential for the rougher
parts of life and the challenge to come.

There's nothing analytic here about yearning; it is manifest in every detail. *I yearn not only for a literal home but also for
a place in the world*—a lack reflected in the empty landscape.

The yearning finds its way, in a certain kind of irony, into her memories. The sounds of the train metaphorically echo the rending of her old life. The dynamic is working on all those levels at once, all reflecting the same yearning.

Here's the opening of a short story, "Brownsville," from a book called *Blues and Trouble* by Tom Piazza. Again, the yearning comes out of beautiful moment-to-moment sensual details, all fit organically together.

> I've been trying to get to Brownsville, Texas, for weeks. Right now it's a hundred degrees in New Orleans and the gays are running down Chartres Street with no shirts on, trying to stay young. I'm not running anymore. When I get to Brownsville I'm going to sit down in the middle of the street, and that will be the end of the line.
>
> Ten in the morning and they're playing a Schubert piano trio on the tape and the breeze is blowing in from the street and I'm sobbing into a napkin. "L. G.," she used to say, "you think I'm a mess? You're a mess, too, L. G." That was a consolation to her.
>
> The walls in this café have been stained by patches of seeping water that will never dry, and the plaster has fallen away in swatches that look like countries nobody's ever heard of. Pictures of Napoleon are all over the place: Napoleon blowing it at Waterloo, Napoleon holding his dick on St. Helena, Napoleon sitting in some subtropical café thinking about the past, getting drunk, plotting revenge.

I picture Brownsville as a place under a merciless sun, where one-eyed dogs stand in the middle of dusty, empty streets staring at you and hot breeze blows inside your shirt and there's nowhere to go. It's always noon, and there are no explanations required. I'm going to Brownsville exactly because I've got no reason to go there. Anybody asks me why Brownsville—there's no fucking answer. That's why I'm going there.

Last night I slept with a woman who had hair down to her ankles and a shotgun in her bathtub and all the mirrors in her room rattled when she laughed. She was good to me; I'll never say a bad word about her. There's always a history, though; her daughter was sleeping on a blanket in the dining room. It would have been per-fect except for that.

The past keeps rising up here; the water table is too high. All around the Quarter groups of tourists float like clumps of sewage.

"I've been trying to get to Brownsville, Texas, for weeks. Right now it's a hundred degrees in New Orleans." This goal of getting to Brownsville provides a dynamic from the begin-ning. He says the gays are trying to stay young, but "I'm not running anymore." Hmmm—he's not running but he's trying to get to Brownsville; is there some sort of contradiction there? He feels he's getting old, nothing has seemed to work for him. He has a failed past, like Napoleon, whose history certainly contained a huge and final failure. His immediate failure is this breakup with someone—who used to say that he's a mess.

Well, he's a mess. And notice the walls of the café: . . . sil-
houettes of "countries nobody's ever heard of." His life is as
meaningless as that; nobody's heard of him, and he's going
someplace anonymous, where you don't have to explain anything, because he has no explanations. His own past is likened
to Napoleon—"blowing it at Waterloo . . . holding his dick
on St. Helena . . . sitting in some subtropical café," which is
where our narrator is sitting at the moment, getting drunk.
Napoleon was plotting his revenge. In this, he's different from
our narrator, who isn't "running anymore." But we know that
Napoleon's revenge never came, don't we? He's critical of
Napoleon for this. He thinks he wants to go to a place where
it's always noon, no explanations are required, you just sit in
a hot breeze under the sun. That's what he thinks he wants,
but—a lot of modern fiction works with dramatic irony—we
know more than the narrator does.

Then, we move to a woman he slept with last night, and
what wonderful details he has of her: hair down to her ankles,
shotgun in her bathtub, the mirrors in her room rattling when
she laughs. "She was always good to me." What is it that makes
the whole imperfect? Her child sleeping in the other room—
which is what? Her past. The tension lies between *here I am*
and *the past is fucked,* just like the water table that keeps rising in this town that has too much past.

What is his yearning? The dramatic irony here is that
he seems to be yearning to disconnect from his failed past. But
he's sobbing into his napkin; he slept with this woman just
last night, and everything was fine except for this goddamned
past. If he could just be in the present. In fact, he yearns to

connect. The yearning for disconnection is really an emotional inverse; this is why he's chosen Brownsville, where it is always "noon." He's not so close to wanting oblivion as he would have himself believe.

Here's another opening passage, this one from "The Bog Man," a short story from *Wilderness Tips* by Margaret Atwood.

> Julie broke up with Connor in the middle of a swamp.
>
> Julie silently revises: not exactly in the middle, not knee-deep in rotting leaves and dubious brown water. More or less on the edge; sort of within striking distance. Well, in an inn, to be precise. Well, not even an inn. A room in a pub. What was available.
>
> And not in a swamp anyway. In a bog. *Swamp* is when the water goes in one end and out the other, *bog* is when it goes in and stays in. How many times did Connor have to explain the difference? Quite a few. But Julie prefers the sound of the word *swamp*. It is mistier, more haunted. *Bog* is a slang word for *toilet,* and when you hear *bog* you know the toilet will be a battered and smelly one, and that there will be no toilet paper.
>
> So Julie always says: *I broke up with Connor in the middle of a swamp.*
>
> There are other things she revises as well. She revises Connor. She revises herself. Connor's wife stays approximately the same, but she was an invention of Julie's in the first place, since Julie never met her. Sometimes she used to wonder whether the wife really existed at all,

or was just a fiction of Connor's, useful for keeping Julie at arm's length. But, no, the wife existed all right. She was solid, and she became more solid as time went on.

Connor mentioned the wife, and the three children, and the dog, fairly soon after he and Julie met. Well, not met. Slept together. It was almost the same thing.

Julie supposes, now, that he didn't want to scare her off by bringing up the subject too soon. She herself was only twenty, and too naïve to even think of looking for clues, such as the white circle on the ring finger. By the time he did get round to making a sheepish avowal or confession, Julie was in no position to be scared off. She was already lying in a motel room, wound loosely in a sheet. She was too tired to be scared off and also too amazed, and also too grateful. Connor was not her first lover but he was her first grown-up one, he was the first who did not treat sex as some kind of panty raid. He took her body seriously, which impressed her to no end.

Understand that in everything I'm reading you, there's an organic coherence among the details, built around a character with a dynamic yearning. Julie's yearning begins to manifest itself how?—by revising everything. Everything is qualified. She makes a statement, revises it, backs out of it, deromanticizes it. But then returns to it. At once, we see this inner conflict going on. She wants to uplift, to rewrite romantically; then she wants to debunk, to go back and see things with brutal clarity. And this process keeps repeating. *More or less. Sort of. To be precise.*

Well, not even. What was available. Well, not met. Slept together. Ultimately, there's a moment when we learn what has kept her with that married man: he took her body seriously.

The point of revision is to find meaning. You revise to clarify the meaning of something. You understand, I'm doing this terrible artificial thing, to be forgotten instantly, giving you a little analytical summary to show what's going on here in the moment. The moment is the point: her attachment to Connor comes from the moment she knew that he took her body seriously. The yearning is to find meaning and appropriate relevance in her life.

The last example is from James Joyce's story, "The Sisters," from *Dubliners*.

> There was no hope for him this time: it was the third stroke. Night after night I had passed the house (it was vacation time) and studied the lighted square of window: and night after night I had found it lighted in the same way, faintly and evenly. If he was dead, I thought, I would see the reflection of candles on the darkened blind, for I knew that two candles must be set at the head of a corpse. He had often said to me, "I am not long for this world," and I had thought the words idle. Now I knew they were true. Every night as I gazed up at the window I said softly to myself the word *paralysis*. It had always sounded strangely in my ears, like the word *gnomon* in the Euclid and the word *simony* in the Catechism. But now it sounded to me like the name of some maleficent and sinful being. It filled me with fear, and

yet I longed to be nearer to it and to look upon its deadly work.

At home he learns of the old man's death:

"Well, so your old friend is gone, you'll be sorry to hear."

"Who?" said I.

"Father Flynn."

"Is he dead?"

"Mr. Cotter here has just told us. He was passing by the house."

I knew that I was under observation, so I continued eating as if the news had not interested me. My uncle explained to old Cotter.

"The youngster and he were great friends. The old chap taught him a great deal, mind you; and they say he had a great wish for him."

"God have mercy on his soul," said my aunt piously.

Old Cotter looked at me for a while. I felt that his little beady black eyes were examining me, but I would not satisfy him by looking up from the plate. He returned to his pipe and finally spat rudely into the grate.

"I wouldn't like children of mine," he said, "to have too much to say to a man like that."

"How do you mean, Mr. Cotter?" asked my aunt.

"What I mean is," said old Cotter, "it's bad for children. My idea is: let a young lad run about and play with young lads of his own age and not be . . . am I right, Jack?"

It seems to me evident from the very first sentences what this young man's yearning is. A man is dying, and our narrator has carefully watched the process "night after night." The passion, the yearning, is in that phrase instantly. It's vacation time, and this time the old man has suffered "the third stroke," and our narrator is still walking past that window, studying the lighted square of the window "night after night." Of course, the deep connection the dying man has with our narrator is immediately clear as well. "He had often said to me, 'I am not long for this world,' and I had thought the words idle." The suggestion of an ongoing relationship—that the dying man had been his adviser and confidant, and even that the narrator had taken his words with a grain of salt—all represents a kind of intimacy between them. The impact of this man's process of dying is clear, too, in the words our narrator repeats to himself. The deep connection, as it turns out, between the narrator and this priest, and the institution and worldview with its mysteries that the priest represents, is reflected in our narrator's focus on the words that he says softly to himself, not only in the "paralysis" that the man of God now suffers, but in the definition of *gnomon*, which is "an interpreter, a pointer," and *simony*, which is the buying and selling of religious pardons. These words take on a kind of personality, as he says that the words sounded to him like "some maleficent and sinful being."

When the narrator gets home, he keeps his own counsel and is very quiet, but he is critical of the adults that surround him, his aunt and uncle and old Cotter. The adults contend that you can learn too much; that you really need not pay attention to the dark and serious things of the world; that, as Cotter says, education is bad for children because their minds are so impressionable. All of this adds up organically, and deepens our understanding of the boy whose hunger for learning, and knowledge of the darkness and the seriousness of the world, whose very impressionability leads us to identify with him.

I caution you once again to understand that this is a secondary and artificial way of responding to literature, and that this philosophical articulation of these characters' yearning runs counter to the ways in which we are meant to and do respond to them in a story. But here our narrator *yearns* for the truth. He's going night after night past the window, reading the implications of what sort of candles are lit and working through the mysteries of religion in terms of where this man may be headed when he dies. The narrator yearns to face the dark things honestly. He's doing so in a world commanded by adults who would keep him ignorant, who would prevent him from knowing, much less speaking, the truth. And this yearning is inherent in every detail of image, of voice, moment by moment in the narrator's experience.

4

CINEMA OF THE MIND

"If only we could pull out our brains and use only our eyes."
—*Pablo Picasso*

Fiction technique and film technique have a great deal in common. We're not talking here tonight about how to translate a book to the screen or how a film could be transformed into a novel, but about deep and essential common ground.

The great D. W. Griffith (I say *great* in the sense of moviemaker; he was a loathsome human being)—who did those massive silent screen epics in the teens of the last century, *Intolerance* and *The Birth of a Nation*—was rightly credited with inventing modern film technique. Griffith himself credited one man with teaching him everything he knew about film, and that was Charles Dickens. Of course, Dickens died several decades before film was invented, but what Griffith learned from him about this new art form of the twentieth century goes to the heart of the experience of reading literature.

Pause for a moment and consider what goes on within you when you read a wonderful work of fiction. The experience is, in fact, a kind of cinema of the inner consciousness. When you read a work of literature, the characters and the setting and the actions are evoked as images, as a kind of dream in your consciousness, are they not? The primary senses—sight and sound—prevail, just as in the cinema, but in addition to seeing and hearing, you experience taste and smell, you can feel things on your skin as the narrative moves through your consciousness. This is omnisensual cinema. Consequently, it makes sense that the techniques of literature are those we understand to be filmic.

All of the techniques that filmmakers employ, and which you understand intuitively as filmgoers, have direct analogies in fiction. And because fiction writers are the writer-directors of the cinema of inner consciousness, you will need to develop the techniques of film as well. I want to deal with some of those techniques tonight, because I think they can help you overcome some of the problems I've been describing in the past few weeks: the impulse for abstraction and analysis, for summary and generalization, problems of rhythm and transition—how to get from one scene to another or one image to another or one sentence to another—how to put all the parts together, where to place your own personal focus when you're in your own creative trance.

I inveigh against abstraction in these works called novels and stories. Consider how Jack Nicholson as a crotchety old bachelor in a movie looks at Helen Hunt. We see his face on the screen; he lifts an eyebrow; his lip curls. If the screen suddenly went blank and the word "wryly" came up, or "sarcasm," or "contempt," how would you react? You can imagine: with great discomfort. For readers who know how to read, abstraction, generalization, analysis, and interpretation have the same deleterious effect.

Let's turn to a few basic film concepts, most of which will be familiar to you, and then let's look at some literature together and see how it is that writers have always been filmmakers.

The *shot* is the basic building block of film. From your point of view as spectator, the shot is a unit of uninterrupted flow of imagery. From the moment that image begins to whenever that image is interrupted, by whatever—that is the shot. That is the basis of every film.

Then there are a number of transitional devices for getting from one shot to another. By far the most common, used for the vast majority of transitions, is the *cut*. You see an image on the screen, and snap! it's not there; another image is there in its place. It's called a cut because originally when film was edited—and this has only changed in the last few years—the film stock was literally cut and then spliced together with the image that followed.

And, of course, shots are connected into scenes and scenes are developed into sequences. *Scenes* are unified actions occurring in a single time and place—maybe a single shot, more likely a group of shots. A *sequence* is a group of scenes comprising a dramatic segment of a film.

These concepts describe not only the inevitable flow of film but also the narrative voice as picture maker. These pictures have a life in time. They begin, they develop, and they end in equivalents of the filmic concepts. As in film, it is the manipulation of these "shots" accumulating into "scenes" and "sequences" that creates meaning and produces the rhythm of the voice of the narrator.

The narrative voice in fiction is always adjusting our view of the physical world it creates, which is equivalent to another group of film techniques on a continuum from extreme *long shot* to extreme *close-up*, and the many stages in between. The long shot, the *medium shot*, the close-up, the extreme close-up—you can slice that sausage as fine as you wish. The narrative voice always places our reader's consciousness at a certain distance from the images it's creating. It can place us at a far distance or bring us into a position of intimate proximity by its choice of detail, by what it lets through the camera lens.

Not only do fiction and film adjust us in terms of our physical relationship to the image, they are also constantly adjusting our sense of time. Fiction and film both often speed time up or slow it down, operating in *slow motion* and *fast motion*. You're familiar with the moment when the lovers are finally reunited and they run to each other in slow motion across the plaza or the meadow. In the late sixties or early seventies Sam Peckinpah invented slow-motion violence—at the end of the Western *The Wild Bunch*, for example, when a gang of criminals all get blown away in excruciating slow motion. That technique has by now become a filmic cliché: every bullet's impact is in lugubrious slow motion.

Fast motion in film, however, is almost always comic in effect. Some filmmakers have tried to overcome the comic uses of fast motion, but without much success. A wonderful and deadly serious early silent film, *Nosferatu*, has a sequence in fast motion when Nosferatu's coffin arrives from abroad and is taken off the ship and carried into the hearse—and it looks comic. I can't think of an example in modern filmmaking where fast motion is used except for comic effect. In fiction, though, fast motion can be used with an infinite variety of emotional nuance.

The last film technique I want to lay on the table for you is one of the most crucial. It's called *montage*. Montage is a concept developed by Sergey Eisenstein, a great Russian early film director. Simply put, montage creates meaning by placing two things next to each other, juxtaposing elements. In a work of art everything is laden with affect, and whenever you put two of *anything* next to each other, a third thing emerges; that's what montage is about. If you see an image on the screen of a grassy slope and a freshly dug and refilled grave, and we cut to a woman in black walking slowly down a gravel path beneath some trees, the montage leads you instantly to understand that this woman has left a loved one in the grave she just visited. In film the juxtaposed elements are most often visual, but in fiction the flexibility is almost infinite.

Let's look at some examples now. I'm going to start with a piece from a short story by Hemingway, "Cat in the Rain." I want you to just listen to the flow here of Hemingway's narrative voice, and then we'll come back to it and examine it in cinematic terms.

> The American wife stood at the window looking out. Outside right under their window a cat was crouched under one of the dripping green tables. The cat was trying to make herself so compact that she would not be dripped on.

"I'm going down and get that kitty," the American wife said.

"I'll do it," her husband offered from the bed.

"No, I'll get it. The poor kitty out trying to keep dry under a table."

The husband went on reading, lying propped up with the two pillows at the foot of the bed.

"Don't get wet," he said.

"The American wife stood at the window looking out." Hemingway here evokes the full figure of the wife standing at the window. In interior terms, it's a kind of medium long shot. We see her fully from across the room.

"Outside right under their window a cat was crouched under one of the dripping green tables." What has happened here? We have now cut to what she is seeing. You understand this same technique when you're watching a movie: in *Out of Africa*, you see Robert Redford's face on the screen. He looks. Cut. We now see a lion bounding toward the camera. We understand that this is what he is seeing because of that montage: Robert Redford's face, a lion coming this way; and the third thing emerges. The most deprived, illiterate youngster understands this.

Hemingway has just used the same technique. "The American wife stood at the window looking out," and "Outside right under their window a cat was crouched under one of the dripping green tables." We see that cat, again in a kind of medium long shot, the table and the rain and the cat underneath. How many inexperienced writers, having written

"The American wife stood at the window looking out," and now wanting us to understand what she's seeing, are going to put her back into the next sentence? "The American wife stood at the window looking out. She watched a cat crouching under one of the dripping green tables." Right? You now have a slack, awkward run of prose. It is as if, in the film, we see Robert Redford's face on the screen. Cut. Now we see the lion bounding this way, but in the foreground is the back of Robert Redford's head. Can you imagine the awkwardness of that shot? Yet we all write sentences with that kind of built-in awkwardness, when we don't need "her" in the sentence; montage takes care of it much more elegantly and powerfully.

"Outside right under their window a cat was crouched under one of the dripping green tables. The cat was trying to make herself so compact that she would not be dripped on." What just happened? We zoom in for a close-up on the cat.

" 'I'm going down and get that kitty,' the American wife said." How many times in film have you seen an image, and then a line of dialogue, somebody's voice coming in over that image, and then an image of the speaker? Images linger and other images come in on top. This is all happening very fast, but I promise you it's happening as you read, and it's exactly what Hemingway does here. The dialogue tag doesn't come until the end; first it's a voice, then we know who speaks. There's an after-image of the cat until Hemingway puts in the character.

" 'I'll do it,' her husband offered from the bed." Notice that we don't have any equivalent to "The American wife stood at the window." We know he's on the bed but don't know what his physical position is; we do not see him fully, and so for the moment it's a close up of him as he speaks.

" 'No, I'll get it. The poor kitty out trying to keep dry under a table.' " No dialogue tag this time. So we stay with him as her voice floats through. We know it's her because of the conventions of paragraphing in dialogue. But our attention is not brought back to her. We stay with him, and we're still close on him. And then, the husband "went on reading, lying propped up with the two pillows at the foot of the bed." The camera pulls back slowly, revealing him finally in full figure, reading and lying propped up at the foot of the bed. " 'Don't get wet,' he said."

When I read that, a number of you smiled. Why? Because he has not moved a muscle. You do not have to say, *I'll do it," her husband offered insincerely from the bed*. You do not need to abstract that, because all of the affect is embedded in the cinematically sensual way Hemingway directs the scene. The revelation comes through montage. The husband says "I'll do it," we see him lying there doing nothing, and next comes, "Don't get wet." It's raining out; of course she's going to get wet.

So much is said about the relationship in so few words!—because Hemingway was a brilliant filmmaker.

Fast action, slow motion: what I want to show you now is how these venerable film techniques have always worked for us writers of narrative. This passage is from the Book of Judges, twenty-five hundred years old. The Old Testament—King James Version, of course. The passage is self-explanatory except for the character of Sisera—a bad guy who's bringing his armies to face Israel.

Blessed above women shall Jael the wife of Heber the Kenite be; blessed shall she be above women in the tent.

He asked water, and she gave him milk; she brought forth butter in a lordly dish.

She put her hand to the nail, and her right hand to the workmen's hammer; and with the hammer she smote Sisera, she smote off his head, when she had pierced and stricken through his temples.

At her feet he bowed, he fell, he lay down: at her feet, he bowed, he fell: where he bowed, there he fell down dead.

The mother of Sisera looked out at a window, and cried through the lattice, Why is his chariot so long in coming?

This is utterly cinematic: ". . . he bowed, he fell, he lay down: at her feet, he bowed, he fell: where he bowed, there he fell down dead." That is slow-motion violence à la Sam Peckinpah. He is falling forever. And then that wonderful cut, that wonderful bit of montage, *sans* transitional device: ". . . he fell down dead"; "The mother of Sisera looked out at a window . . ." You can see the latticework, the shadow of it on her face. "Why is his chariot so long in coming?" He should be finished raping and pillaging by now. Time for dinner.

Next I want to read you a little bit of Henry James with some ellipses in it. I want to give you a cheek-by-jowl example of three speeds in a brief section of "The Siege of London." Here is an example of appropriate summary—I've used *summary* as an epithet in these lectures, but the summary that's destructive races through what needs to be done in the moment; it is summary that has no sensual impact on the reader. Sensual, carefully and judiciously used summary can be effective and, indeed, is how you mostly achieve fast motion—fast action—in fiction.

The "glass" referred to here is an opera glass; that is, a little pair of binoculars.

> That solemn piece of upholstery, the curtain of the Comédie Française, had fallen upon the first act of the piece, and our two Americans had taken advantage of the interval to pass out of the huge, hot theatre, in company with the other occupants of the stalls . . .
>
> She turned . . . and presented her face to the public—a fair, well-drawn face, with smiling eyes, smiling lips, ornamented over the brow with delicate rings of black hair and, in each ear, with the sparkle of a diamond sufficiently large to be seen across the Théâtre Français . . .
>
> Littlemore looked at her, then abruptly he gave an exclamation. "Give me the glass!"
>
> "Do you know her?" his companion asked, as he directed the little instrument.
>
> Littlemore made no answer; he only looked in silence; then he handed back the glass. "No, she's not respectable," he said. And he dropped into his seat again. As Waterville remained standing, he added, "Please sit down; I think she saw me."

Now this is the great thing about fiction. We can move from fast action to slow motion to real time seamlessly and with great nuance. The first part of that was fast action—"that solemn piece of upholstery"—it's summary but with wonderful sensual impact—*that heavy, roughly textured thing*. ". . . the curtain of the Comédie Française, had fallen upon the first act . . . and our two Americans had taken advantage of the interval to pass out of the huge, hot theatre, in company with the other occupants of the stalls." He never lets go of the image in our minds but we move quickly. Then time stops. We examine her face in very slow motion. "She turned . . . and presented her face to the public," and there's this lovely little bit of close examination: ". . . a fair, well-drawn face, with smiling eyes, smiling lips, ornamented over the brow with delicate rings of black hair and, in each ear, with the sparkle of a diamond . . ." Then we shift into real time, the moment-to-moment time that is your normal speed as fiction writers. The *normal* speed, I emphasize.

"Littlemore looked at her, then abruptly he gave an exclamation. 'Give me the glass!'" We watch him sit down. We watch the handing of the glass. We hear the words of their exchange. It's all in real time there.

Next I'm going to give an example from the writer who taught D. W. Griffith everything he knew about film. This is the opening of the novel *Great Expectations* by Charles Dickens. Our narrator, Philip Pirrip, is writing in his adulthood, looking back to his childhood as an orphan, and he refers to himself sometimes in the third person, sometimes in the first person. During his childhood he was called Pip. The

people mentioned here are his dead siblings and his parents.
Just go to the movies:

> Ours was the marsh country, down by the river,
> within, as the river wound, twenty miles of the sea. My
> first most vivid and broad impression of the identity
> of things seems to me to have been gained on a memo-
> rable raw afternoon towards evening. At such a time I
> found out for certain that this bleak place overgrown
> with nettles was the churchyard; and that Philip Pirrip,
> Late of the Parish, and Also Georgiana Wife of the
> Above, were dead and buried; and that Alexander,
> Bartholomew, Abraham, Tobias, and Roger, infant chil-
> dren of the aforesaid, were also dead and buried; and that
> the dark flat wilderness beyond the churchyard, inter-
> sected with dikes and mounds and gates, with scattered
> cattle feeding on it, was the marshes; and that the low
> leaden line beyond was the river; and that the distant
> savage lair from which the wind was rushing was the sea;
> and that the small bundle of shivers growing afraid of it
> all and beginning to cry was Pip.
>
> "Hold your noise!" cried a terrible voice, as a man
> started up from among the graves at the side of the
> church porch. "Keep still, you little devil, or I'll cut your
> throat!"
>
> A fearful man, all in coarse gray, with a great iron
> on his leg. A man with no hat, and with broken shoes,
> and with an old rag tied round his head. A man who had
> been soaked in water, and smothered in mud, and lamed

by stones, and cut by flints, and stung by nettles, and
torn by briars; who limped, and shivered, and glared and
growled; and whose teeth chattered in his head as he
seized me by the chin.

"Oh, don't cut my throat, sir," I pleaded in terror.
"Pray don't do it, sir."

"Tell us your name," said the man. "Quick!"

"Pip, sir."

"Once more," said the man, staring at me. "Give
it mouth!"

"Pip. Pip, sir."

"Show us where you live," said the man. "Pint out
the place!"

I pointed to where our village lay, on the flat in-
shore, among the alder-trees and pollards, a mile or more
from the church.

The man, after looking at me for a moment, turned
me upside down, and emptied my pockets. There was
nothing in them but a piece of bread. When the church
came to itself—for he was so sudden and strong that he
made it go head over heels before me, and I saw the
steeple under my feet—when the church came to itself,
I say, I was seated on a high tombstone, trembling, while
he ate the bread ravenously.

Dickens begins with what they call the *establishing shot*.
We're at "a memorable raw afternoon towards evening. At
such a time I found out for certain that this bleak place overgrown with nettles was the churchyard . . ." We get a long shot

in the gathering dark of the churchyard. And then, what does Dickens do? He cuts to close-ups and pans one after another along the tombstones—as we can tell from the formal phrasing "Late of the parish":

> . . . that Philip Pirrip, Late of the Parish, and Also Georgiana Wife of the Above, were dead and buried; and that Alexander, Bartholomew, Abraham, Tobias, and Roger, infant children of the aforesaid, were also dead and buried.

These are, in fact, the graves of Pip's dead father, his dead mother, and dead brother, dead brother, dead brother, dead brother, dead brother—one after another.

You see the absolutely essential quality of fiction-as-film when you see what he does then. We go from that last dead brother to what?

> . . . and that the dark flat wilderness beyond the churchyard, intersected with dikes and mounds and gates, with scattered cattle feeding on it, was the marshes . . .

He lifts his camera from the dead brother and looks off to a long shot out over the mounds and gates and dikes to the marshes, beyond the churchyard, and then where?

> . . . and that the low, leaden line beyond was the river . . .

Then we go to an even longer shot:

. . . and that the distant savage lair from which the wind
was rushing was the sea . . .

He takes us to an extreme shot at the farthest horizon.
Then what? He cuts from that distant horizon to a close-up
of the orphan child, the narrator of our novel, "the small
bundle of shivers growing afraid of it all and beginning to
cry was Pip."
How many writers would do this, with perfect logic?

> My first most vivid and broad impression of the
> identity of things seems to me to have been gained on a
> memorable raw afternoon towards evening. At such a
> time I found out for certain that this bleak place over-
> grown with nettles was the churchyard; and that Philip
> Pirrip, Late of the Parish, and Also Georgiana Wife of
> the Above, were dead and buried; and that Alexander,
> Bartholomew, Abraham, Tobias, and Roger, infant chil-
> dren of the aforesaid, were also dead and buried; and that
> the small bundle of shivers growing afraid of it all and
> beginning to cry was Pip.

Perfectly logical. Perfectly thoughtful. Dead father, dead
mother, dead brother, dead brother, dead brother, dead
brother, dead brother, last remaining child of the family.
Montage, of course. But in such a novel, where you went
from the last dead brother to the remaining child, you would
be in a totally different world from the one that Dickens is
creating. You would be in a world where the focus is on the

plight of an orphan, a family in trouble—a sociological problem, a sentimental tale of a struggling child.

Dickens's world is about something far greater, and Pip
does not yearn for a family; he yearns for his destiny. When
you move from that last dead child to the marshes and the river
and to the far horizon, and the whole sensual world is bleak
and empty and mysterious, and there's a dark wind blowing
from that far horizon, and *then* you cut to the child—that montage creates something utterly different, a world in which the
issue is not just, "Gosh, I don't have parents. I'm a kid struggling," but "I am a human soul trying to work out the destiny
of my existence."

Let's go further.

> "Hold your noise!" cried a terrible voice, as a man
> started up from among the graves at the side of the church
> porch. "Keep still, you little devil, or I'll cut your throat!"

How does Pip respond to this? "'Oh, don't cut my throat,
sir,' I pleaded in terror. . . ." Now, I don't mean to presume to
edit Charles Dickens, but Dickens sometimes wrote in haste.
Does he really need to say "in terror"? Do you understand what
I'm talking about in terms of abstractions? Certainly the world
of emotional abundance he's creating can tolerate these extra
taps on the knee, but they are not necessary. Pip's terror is
manifest already, is it not?

But the important thing to understand here is that the
man says, "I'll cut your throat," and Pip says, "Don't cut my
throat." How long do you think it took him to come to that

response? A nanosecond. And how is it written? Pay attention, because there's something really interesting about these three sentences:

> . . . "Keep still, you little devil, or I'll cut your throat!"
>
> A fearful man, all in coarse gray, with a great iron on his leg. A man with no hat, and with broken shoes, and with an old rag tied around his head. A man who had been soaked in water, and smothered in mud, and lamed by stones, and cut by flints, and stung by nettles, and torn by briars; who limped, and shivered, and glared and growled; and whose teeth chattered in his head as he seized me by the chin.
>
> "Oh, don't cut my throat, sir," . . .

Time stops here, doesn't it? This is *extreme* slow motion, because all of that comes between "I'm going to cut your throat" and "Oh, don't . . ." What is the psychological reality of that? When was the last time you skidded your car on a wet pavement? What happens? You hear every beat of your heart; that telephone pole is floating in your direction, in extreme slow motion, right? It is absolutely organically appropriate for time to slow down drastically in a moment of terror like that. And remember I'm talking about the organic nature of art; every tiny sensual detail has to resonate into everything else. What's unusual about those three sentences in that paragraph where time has stopped? I bet most of you didn't even notice that not one of them is a complete sentence. Listen to it again:

A fearful man, all in coarse gray, with a great iron on his leg. A man with no hat, and with broken shoes, and with an old rag tied round his head. ["Tied round his head" is a subordinate clause here.] A man who had been soaked in water, and smothered in mud, and lamed by stones, and cut by flints, and stung by nettles, and torn by briars; who limped, and shivered, and glared and growled; and whose teeth chattered in his head as he seized me by the chin.

There's not a single independent verb in those three sentences. Why? Time has stopped. What are the parts of speech that signify the passage of time? Active verbs. Things happen. But here nothing is happening except perception. It is beautifully appropriate—and you don't even notice, except afterward, in an analytic way.

The organic nature of art, down to syntax.

We've dealt so far with very clear examples, I think, of the correspondence of film and fiction techniques, but there are many, many others. I daresay that if you examine the tiniest filmic concept, the most subtle, nuanced filmic concept, you can find its equivalence in fiction.

I want to leave you with one more example, a subtle one, but I think an unmistakable one: the common transitional device called *dissolve*. The dissolve is a transition from one image to another where the first fades while the second comes into focus superimposed over the first. The two things, then, mix inextricably for a time.

I want to give you an example of dissolve from my own work—a novel hardly ever read by anybody, called *Wabash*. I need to give you some background first. Deborah and Jeremy Cole live in the fictional steel mill town of Wabash, Illinois. It's 1932. They're both struggling with private demons of one sort or another. He's getting involved in radical politics at the steel mill where he works; she's trying to reconcile a family of women who rip each other to pieces as a matter of daily course. But Jeremy and Deborah carry a shared grief that has been a barrier in their marriage for some time—the death of their little girl, Lizzy, who died from pneumonia a couple of years before. They have not made love since Lizzy died. They do not touch. There's no intimacy between them at all. In this scene they go off for a picnic on an ancient Indian burial mound, a gesture toward reconciliation, trying to find moments when they can reconnect. But as the scene progresses, they lapse into separate memories about their daughter, memories that are lovely but painful.

The scene partly represents a technical problem—not, I need hardly stress anymore, that I was conscious of finding a technical solution to an analytically perceived problem. This is analysis after the fact. But the problem was that I wrote the book in the third-person limited omniscient, with two point-of-view characters, Deborah and Jeremy. In the sections that begin in Jeremy's sensibility, the narrator has no access to Deborah. And in the sections that begin with Deborah, the narrator has no access to Jeremy. This is so for the first eighty-some pages of the book. But in this scene of the picnic, just as they aspire to come together—so does the narrator get into both sensibilities at the same time. The narrator moves between these two isolated reveries, hoping to bring them together somehow.

A couple of things you need to know: the memory that Deborah has is of seeing Lizzy outside the house one day crouching near the grass, swaying in front of a poisonous copperhead snake, singing a variation of the old nursery rhyme "Hush little snaky, don't you cry." The copperhead is swaying and coiling as well; Lizzy has literally charmed the snake.

Jeremy's memory involves Lizzy and his work at the steel mill. He has Lizzy on his shoulders. It's nighttime. He's stopped near the slag pile and has an unobstructed view of the blast furnace. He's watching its beauty: the flames of the ovens and the billows of smoke, the constellation of lights on the equipment, and a single prominent smokestack that is flaring off a flame from the excess gasses.

Here is the passage that uses the technique of the dissolve:

Deborah waited motionless as Lizzy sang to the snake and finally Deborah whispered, Come away now, and her daughter rose slowly and left the copperhead where it lay charmed on the grass and when Lizzy was near, Deborah grasped her hand and Jeremy reached up to grasp his daughter's hand and she said, What's that jelly fire? and he looked and he knew at once what she meant—the flame coming from the tall, thin stack. It's a bleeder valve, he said, and he felt her chin touch the top of his head; he could imagine her resting her head on his so that she could study this beautiful flame and when Lizzy looked up at her mother she smiled a smile that seemed full of some special knowledge and Lizzy's thoughtful study of the flame and her smile at the charming of the snake brought both Jeremy and Deborah to the same tremor of grief. They each felt it in the other's body and to feel the other's grief was too much to add to their own and they pulled gently apart. Jeremy rose and walked to the western edge of the mound and he looked off to the mill and Deborah lay flat and closed her eyes against the sky and she thought she heard a gliding nearby in the grass but she did not care and did not move.

Did you hear the dissolve? It's set up with Lizzy's question, "What's that jelly fire?" and Jeremy knows at once what she means. Focus on "He could imagine her resting her head on his so that she could study this beautiful flame and when Lizzy looked up at her mother . . ." Now we are in his reverie, and for a moment there the two images are superimposed because the "looking up" we first take to mean Lizzy looking up from her father's head toward that bleeder valve; but then we realize it's with her mother. "And when Lizzy looked up." It's even tapped a little bit, because it is linked to the same gesture that Jeremy made to look in the same direction. So we have a clear sense of her looking up at the flame while she's with Jeremy and then all of a sudden she's also looking at her mother. Then we adjust to seeing her looking up only at her mother. And so one dissolves into the other. After this, the narrative voice goes back for a long while into the two separate sensibilities. So the flowing together in the narrative voice has a kind of ironic sadness to it, which resonates in the detail, because it gives a sense of what could happen between these two people but, in fact, does not.

So I urge you as fiction writers to recognize that the nature of the process you're working with is filmic. A lot of the problems that I've been articulating for you in the last few weeks can yield to you if you give yourself over to elements that are visual, sensual, transitional. Otherwise, you can get bogged down in the stodgy, unyielding doughiness of abstraction. You try to put the transitions in and explain these things, and the narrative power is lost.

Before I leave you with all this talk of film, I want to borrow one more notion from another art form, music, which you will recognize as relevant to film and also important to fiction. When you're listening to a song, a certain kind of expectation develops—harmonically, or in its key or in its rhythm or in its color—and when that expectation is set up, the moment that gives you chill bumps is when the music cuts against the grain. It suddenly spins the harmonic, shifts the key, varies the rhythm, sets the orchestration askew. Musicians call it the *rub*. Two things rub against each other, and that's what gives it life, the unexpected thing that nevertheless feels just right. And that is what happens, too, in the creation of character. When you are inside your characters' yearnings, whenever they're feeling one way, going in one direction, showing certain attitudes, emotions—open your unconscious to the opposite; cut against the grain. *Rub* the thing that seems predictable.

5

A WRITER PREPARES

"No ideas but in things."
—William Carlos Williams

I want to move on now to suggest a system of predreaming, which I used in its purest form for a novel I published back in 1983 called *Countrymen of Bones* and which I think helped to shape my deep instinctive reactions in the process. But hear me when I say "shape" and "instinctive." Our dreams are not "smart." There is no intellect in this world powerful enough to create a great work of novelistic art. Only the unconscious can fit together the stuff of fiction; the conscious mind cannot.

When I said earlier that you could get away with a certain, carefully managed amount of abstraction and analysis that was *a part of your character's voice*, I put a pistol in your mouth. This is a shotgun. I'm even going to cock the trigger for you. I'm going to teach you a way of getting your sensibility around the daunting prospect of creating such an object as a novel. I can't emphasize strongly enough that this is a dangerous system; it must be used as an aid to your unconscious, your trance. If you let this process draw you into your analytic mind, it will do far more harm than good.

Let me describe two kinds of novelists. First there are those who preplan. They outline. They know the end before they begin. But those who figure out what they're going to say before they begin to say it are utterly lost, because if they adhere to the stages of their plan in a kind of "all right, that's done" sort of way, they will end up writing from their heads, automatically.

Then there's the draft writer, who leads an admirably dismal existence. He starts the same way every other sensual artist does. He's got characters floating in his unconscious. He intuits their yearning. He has attached to them a milieu, a circumstance, perhaps an external moment in the world, some event to block that yearning. These are the basic elements you all have when you start a novel. The draft writer begins a draft for the very purposes I've been talking about; he is rightly afraid of being drawn into his mind and his analytical self. He would never preplan, because that would trap him like literal memory, like a "message," like preconceived ends, and thereby destroy his ability to get into the unconscious. So the draft writer feels the necessity of taking the merest hints to start the novel and then plunging in, making approximations, writing rough, by any and all means continuing to write and write and write through a great sprawling draft. And the draft writer relishes this. "Ah, I've got this mass of stuff, and OK, I've got to do the second draft now and the third and the fourth, and the seventeenth, and that's fine . . ." Great works of art have been created this way, and

I suspect statistically it's the more common way to write a novel. It's done because those artists understand the danger of being sucked into their heads.

But you know what? They're just deferring the problem. Because once you have this great raw sprawling first draft, how do you find that leaner, more coherent second draft? The dangers of analysis are very powerful in that search.

What I'm suggesting instead is this:

You go to your writing space as you would on a day when you're planning to write words. You go into your trance, just as you would if you were writing your new book sentence to sentence. But that's not what you do. Instead you're going to do what I call *dreamstorming*—not brainstorming, dreamstorming. You're going to sit or recline in your writing space in your trance, and you're going to free-float, free-associate, sit with your character, watch your character move around in the potential world of this novel. You're going to dream around in this novel, one level removed from moment-to-moment writing—that is, at the level of scene. You're going to do this for six or eight or ten or twelve weeks, every day. You're going to go into your writing space, you're going to go into your dreamspace, you're going to float around, and you're going to dreamstorm potential scenes in such a novel as this with such characters as these, with such yearnings as these. And you'll try to float everywhere in the novel: beginning, middle, end—all over.

You'll have a pad of paper in front of you (you can do it at your computer if you prefer; I do it by hand on legal pads); you'll make a list. You're going to write down on this legal pad six or eight or ten words, not many more, that represent a potential scene. Just identifiers of scenes. Don't hesitate to put something down, as long as it's coming with a sensual hook. You're going to make sure that every scene you list has come to you with some—and it can be very faint, very fragmentary—but some sensual, concrete hook. A little vision of something, a little smell or taste of something, a little sound of something. Do not trust a scene that presents itself to you as an idea. Each scene must have an even fragmentary vision, some sort of sense impression attached to it.

Then you write down the briefest identifier of that scene. For example: *Lloyd rapes Anna. Darrell ponders his digging trowel*—those were typical identifiers from *Countrymen of Bones*. On a typical day you'll float among a number of possible scenes from different parts of the book. And when a compelling scene comes to you, you might be visited by the draft writer's instinct—you want to start writing the full scene right away. Don't do it. Resist it. Even if that scene is "Wow! It's vivid. It's got, oh man, it's really almost there." You've got the six- or eight-word identifier and you leave it at that. This is coitus interruptus. You float on.

Now, you might find yourself getting into little runs of scenes. This scene provokes an image of another scene and another, possibly in sequence. Well, OK, follow it; that's great. List each one, six or eight words. But as soon as the run peters out, do not force it, do not try to find what goes next.

This is very important: through the whole six or eight or ten or twelve weeks, you do *nothing*—and I emphasize *nothing*—to try to organize, structure, or otherwise manipulate

these scenes. You do not even try to reconcile totally contradictory scenes. *Lloyd rapes Anna; Lloyd thinks of raping Anna
but doesn't.* If you have a fragment of each of those scenes on
two different days, don't reconcile them. Put it all down, all
that contradictory stuff.

Eventually, the law of diminishing returns sets in, the
scenes come more slowly, and one day along about the sixth
or eighth or tenth or twelfth week you find yourself with only
one scene and you say, "Whoa, I'm finished with doing this."

Now you've got what? A hundred and fifty? Two hundred scenes? You may have three hundred. You're ready to go
to the next stage.

Say you have two hundred scenes. You buy yourself two
hundred three-by-five cards—not five-by-seven; you only need
room for a phrase, and you want them to be easy to handle.
Turn the cards horizontal. Write the identifying phrase or set
of words in the center of the card. Write one scene per card.
Now you have two hundred cards with two hundred scenes.

By the way, a word about three-by-five cards. Functional
fixedness can cut both ways. Some of you may have a very
strong association between three-by-five cards and an academic thesis or dissertation or other analytical work. If so, you
may need to change something about them. If you worked with
white three-by-fives in your life of the mind, perhaps you can
use a different color card for your creative work.

So you've overcome any possible negative associations
and you've got your two hundred scenes on two hundred cards.
The next day, you go into your writing space, you clear yourself a tabletop, and you go into your trance. Then you start

flipping through your two hundred cards. Every time you look at a card there's a little sense impression that jumps off the card at you: bing, bing, bing. What are you doing? You're looking for the first good scene in the book—the best point of attack. Narratively, this scene will obviously be near the beginning of events but may not be the first chronologically; the story may have already begun. You find this scene, you put it in the upper left-hand corner of that big empty space. Now you flip your cards. You're in your trance. You flip the cards looking for that second scene. What scene would follow the one in the upper left corner of your table? You find it, you put it up there next to the first, and so forth. At the end of the first day, you've got, for example, eight cards in a row. Pick them up in order. Bind them tight.

The next day, you come into your writing space, you go into your trance, you flip those eight cards. You're reading your book. You lay them out again, upper left-hand corner of your table. Now you're looking for the next scene in your cards, and so forth.

Now, there are a couple of ways to go here. Let me deal first with the possibility that you're going to go all the way through to the end of the book, arranging your cards, plotting your whole novel this way. I did that with *Countrymen of Bones* (and in the process my two hundred cards resolved themselves into ninety-two).

What happens as you move along, in your trance, picking up your cards one after the other? Say you get to card number 22—scene number 22—and when you choose the next scene out of the remaining 178, you realize there's a hiatus.

There's a gap in the action between 22 and the next card. Now you can dream up some scenes to fill the gap. Go back into your trance and dream two or three cards in there. At some point you're going to find yourself dreaming, on cue, scenes that you didn't get to the first time, filling gaps. You'll also find that a lot of scenes you *have* dreamed aren't going to make it into the final structure of the novel. And you'll find that the contradictions become reconciled as the structure takes shape and you find your way through to the end. If you're arranging your cards in this extreme way, all the way to the end of the book, number the cards, one to however many represents the whole structure.

During the brainstorming phase, do not give any consideration whatsoever to continuity. Embrace the seeming randomness. If you are tapping into your unconscious and moving around a legitimate character with legitimate yearning, it's hard to say what your unconscious is already perceiving and contextualizing. Once you finish the dreamstorming—weeks—then you try to bring order to that randomness. However, you're simply looking for continuity from one scene to the next. You are looking for the through-line among all those disparate parts. The nature of transition is totally unconsidered. There are so many potential moments and so many possibilities of scene in this book that the only way to explore them fully without willing them into a structure is to let them happen at their own seemingly random pace. Then, only after that, your job is indeed to see the sequence that makes narrative sense of the disparate pieces.

Let me digress for a moment on the subject of research. I always record the books I read on index cards. I'm looking for different things than people look for in academic research, and my cards usually represent a personal index of sense details. Sense details, scenes, images you find in your research you can record on your cards and plug them into the sequence as you arrange. For example, *Countrymen of Bones* was set in the Alamogordo desert during the building of the first atomic bomb. This book took some historical research, as well as reading in nuclear physics and archeology, and the cards allowed me to indicate briefly certain things I might need to know for certain scenes. For example, one of my main characters worked on the bomb, and his job was to lead the team trying to craft the lens in exactly the right shape to hold in the explosion. I didn't have to know everything about the bomb; as soon as I read about the team working on that lens, I said, "That's Lloyd." So I did a lot of indexing of that particular job, the cloud chamber where they tracked the beta particles as they flew off the explosion, the photographs they took of the smoke in the chamber, the track of the beta particle as it poops out. Such details were suggested by scenes in my brainstorming, and some suggested scenes. (For example, Lloyd rearranges a table of cloud chamber photos in a scene.) When you record such details, on your card are just six or eight words, a sense detail, an indicator of scene, or maybe a reference to a book where you can fill in a historical or professional detail. The juice is not written out of these scenes because you've made sure you didn't start writing the description or the dialogue; you just put down the bare indicator and then you went on.

When your cards are arranged, you take the first card and you start writing the novel. Here's the first scene. And it's

ready for your unconscious because all you have here is eight
words, a sense impression to call up that scene. You go into
your trance and you write that scene, and now the second scene
comes up, and you write that scene, and then you write the
third card, and—guess what happens in the third scene. Something you didn't expect. You don't even know where it came
from, because it's coming from your unconscious. Great. That
leads you to a fourth scene and a fifth scene you didn't expect.
Great.

But now you feel that the story has to be drawn back into
the main thrust of everything yet to come. Now that you've
got an unexpected third, fourth, and fifth scene, you go back
and look at the fourth card, and it doesn't fit quite the way it
did at first. *Wait a minute, this changes some things.* In fact, you
must go back and look at all the cards, numbers 4 to 92 (or
however many you have). What do you do now? The next day
you go into your trance and lay out cards 4 to 92 and rearrange
them. In essence, *you rewrite your book structurally.*

I personally write from beginning to end of a book. I don't
want to be dogmatic about this, because I'm sure a particular
artist may do it some other way. But it's hard for me to imagine writing very much out of sequence, because sequence is
crucial in a narrative. If everything is organic in a work of art,
and I skip six or eight or ten scenes to write this scene that
feels hot to me right now, how do I make decisions about character, voice, image, event in that scene? And there are crucial matters of motif, of recomposition, that I will soon speak
of, which are impossible to manage by skipping ahead out of
context. In a contextual vacuum, you make decisions that are

at best tentative. And why are you doing that? I think often-times the impulse is to avert your eyes: *that's the scene I can do safely; the scene that is not really going to challenge me; that's a good scene to write today.*

So I would say it probably doesn't work to "write around" in a novel. Structure happens from the imperatives of the whole object you're creating. When you are driven by the desire for the organic wholeness of the object, and by the need to recompose the elements that are already in the work, and by the dynamics of your character's desire, structure will inevitably come from that.

Yet this system, if it's going to work for you, has to be totally flexible. The fact that you've got ninety-two cards in a row doesn't mean that you're going to write those ninety-two cards out one after the other and think you've got a book. No, you're rewriting and rewriting and rewriting, over and over, not on the level of phrases and paragraphs, but on the level of structure. There's a lot of rewriting going on here, but it's not in drafts, it's in following those instinctive, from-the-hot-spot surprising things, and then restructuring everything to come as a result. It's got to stay flexible, and it's got to stay from the trance, or you will pull the trigger on the shotgun and blow off the back of your novel.

It's also possible to use this system in a more limited, but still more flexible way. In *They Whisper*, my seventh novel, for instance, I was dealing with a very complex structure driven by the flow of delicate emotional associations. No way in hell I could anticipate what the sequence was going to be. But I dreamstormed two hundred cards, and then all I did was look for eight cards that might be near the beginning, and I strung them out and rearranged and rearranged them. Then I wrote those scenes. Once they were exhausted, I went and got six or eight more cards, and so forth. The useful thing was that the possibilities already indicated on the cards helped to guide and structure my unconscious, which was improvising the form as it went.

I've never used the cards the same way twice—maybe they operate for me like a tarot deck. But this is fundamental: keep it open, fluid; realize that nothing you do here is locked in, it's got to stay subordinate to the trance state in order to work.

The advantage I see of this system over multiple drafts is that in the big sprawling rough draft, no matter how open-minded the writer is, she has to make approximations in the first draft, then she must make approximations in the second, and more in the third, adding more rough, headlong stuff in the fourth. If the book is at all complex, the draft writer will hit forks in the road, over and over, and must choose this fork instead of that. If that happens early in the book, or even in the middle, by the time she gets to the end and the novel is sprawling in whatever way it sprawls, it's very difficult to go back and take the other fork she faced on page 30. With this system, all the forks are fine—you follow this one, you follow that one; you go down this fork in the sixth week of dream-storming; in the tenth week, you go down that one, as far as you want to go—because at each point you are rewriting and redreaming the book on the level of structure.

For me, it feels as if this system gives the writer some-thing that she loses doing the draft. But, ultimately you've got to get into your own personal white-hot center and get rid of anything in your process that interferes with that. If it means getting rid of draft writing, you get rid of it; if it means getting rid of dreamstorming, you get rid of that.

If you dreamstorm a short story, you have to understand that the working parts of short stories are not scenes, because most short stories don't have more than a handful of scenes. The working parts are of various sizes and shapes, perhaps a scene but also maybe an image, a fast-forward, a detail, a beat of dialogue. *The lift of an eyebrow* and *Joe rapes Anna*—each of those could be working pieces in the dreamstorming of a short story. Having five cards to represent a structure is not much use to you. You almost have to be a draft writer for short stories.

Still, if you dreamstorm all those various elements, you might try this, which I've done sometimes: you take a legal pad and—maybe there are only three scenes in the story—put your indicator phrase of one at the top, one in the middle, and one toward the bottom. Then all the other elements you've dreamstormed for the story you might plug in under what scenes they may visit. It feels awkward to me, but I came late to writing short stories, after I'd been in my unconscious for a decade and written half a dozen novels from there. But I have talked to writers who have found the card system useful for short stories. It works particularly well for the rare sort of story that covers a long period of time or has a large number of scenes. I've also heard from writers for whom the system gives them impetus in their work; they know better where they're going, what sense details juice their scenes.

Now, how do you make all the pieces fit together? How does something so irrational, so composed of minute details, so thoroughly rooted in the moment-to-moment sense—how does such an object cohere? How does a vision of the human condition emerge from such a thing?

I've already mentioned my premise: that the literary art object is organic and emerges because every sensual detail interlocks with and resonates with every other detail. Everything circles back on itself. The deep patterning of the sensual details mirrors that deep, most patterned level of sense detail in the world. In music it's called motif, and we borrow that term for literature. Things return and return. The associative values of these returning things evolve and interconnect. As a reader you recognize the presence of motif, and as a writer, you create meaning in this way.

At the beginning of the twentieth century acting was understood to be an art form in which an actor intellectually, consciously, willfully—often quite brilliantly, but willfully—took on the gestures, postures, facial expressions, and tone of voice of the character. Then Konstantin Stanislavsky came along to the Moscow Art Theatre and reimagined this art form. He said: No, you do not consciously, analytically put on a performance; that's not where performance comes from. Instead, the actor brings her own internal sense memory, her own sensory mechanism, into internal alignment with the sensory mechanism of the character. Once that has been accomplished, the external performance results. He said: Craft and technique are necessary, but they are secondary. They are downstream from where the performance begins, which is inside you. *Inside you.* This is what came to be called "method acting." It is at the heart of every good performance you see on the television, on the movie screen, on the stage today. Indeed, what I've been talking about with you all along could quite accurately be termed "method writing." It's based on many of the same insights.

There's a teacher named Keith Johnstone, who writes on improvisation and on a process he calls *reincorporating.* People who do improvisation work with disparate elements, some of which may come to them from the audience. Johnstone says the improvising actor is like a man walking backward. He's going forward, but he's doing so constantly with reference to where he's been. The improviser makes progress only by looking back and reincorporating the things that are already present in the narrative.

In a work of fiction those initial disparate, instinctive things come out of your dreamspace. But in writing as in improv—I promise you it's parallel—you cannot move forward narratively by transferring those elements onto your computer screen and saying, "OK, what's next?" Let's go back to Graham Greene and think about the decomposition of your life, that compost heap where all of your experiences have decomposed. Now you wish to compose a work of art. Your unconscious yields up things in an ongoing way, and as a narrator you're looking back always to what's already there. You move forward in a narrative by recomposing, reincorporating the things that are already at work in the story. What you end up with then are the interlocking elements, the return of elements, the motifs that bind everything in the work sensually together. When you do that, a gestalt emerges, a sum that is much greater than those parts. And the work thrums. The thrumming has to do with the interlocking of various tones and sounds and movements of the air.

I want to give you an example. Forgive me, I'm going to go into some detail about that novel, *Countrymen of Bones*— a novel you've almost certainly not read—largely because I have trouble remembering anything else. Did I mention Graham Greene?

Countrymen of Bones, as I said, is set in 1945, mostly in the Alamogordo desert. It's told as a third person narrative with two main point-of-view characters—that is, the narrator has access to two sensibilities. One of them is Darryl Reeves, an archeologist, who has found an Indian burial mound out in the middle of the desert. The mound dates from the seventeenth century, though the desert Indians of the seventeenth century were nomads. So this Indian tribe had to come from the Midwest where the mound builders were. What is it doing here? It's a great archeological find.

Darryl has two grad students working with him, trying to uncover this Indian burial site, and as the book opens they've just cleared the mound away and are about to go into the tableau below the surface of the ground. There are B-29s doing practice bombing nearby, but most important, a thousand yards down the desert south of them, the first atomic bomb is being assembled. The first test is going to happen in fourteen weeks.

The second major character is Lloyd Coulter, a nuclear physicist working on the bomb with J. Robert Oppenheimer, who's a minor character in the book. What we have are two men of the mind, Darryl and Lloyd, scientists who pride themselves on their rationality but who yearn for connection because they are very much disconnected from the world.

I'm going to talk in secondary, artificial ways about this book now, not in the way the book is meant to be encountered.

Each of the men is reining in a potential for violence. Lloyd, particularly, saw his father beat his mother, badly, over and over, and that knowledge roils deep inside him. Darryl seems at first not to have a potential for violence; his problem is disconnectedness, and the devastating loss of a wife who left him several years before.

There's a third major character—not a point-of-view character—Anna Brown, in the Women's Army Corps. She's awakening to her independence, as many women did during the war. Lloyd has encountered her in the supply house of Los Alamos, and he greatly desires her. He arranges for her to be transferred down to the bomb site to work for him. At some point, Darryl also meets Anna and also falls for her. Oppenheimer, sympathetic to the young archaeologist, loans Anna Brown to the excavation site, so an intense jealous rivalry springs up between Lloyd and Darryl.

On one site, then, the atom bomb is being created. On the other, that tableau being uncovered from the earth reveals an Indian king laid out on a cape of twenty thousand polished shell beads—meaning he was a great power. Darryl finds one, then another, and finally a third body within the sacred circle, all three of quite young women whose necks have been broken. It's clear they were ritually murdered to accompany the king to the afterlife.

When the army took over the Alamogordo desert, they put some ranchers off their property. At the very opening of the novel, in addition to the bombs on the horizon, you hear gunfire off to the east because one of those ranchers is holed up there, conducting a kind of guerrilla warfare in rage at having been forced off his ranch.

The book, in its large patterns, is already about violence, is it not? That theme is tapped again when Darryl goes back to Santa Fe and meets a professor who had joined the army, had his back and leg shot off, and who brings rumors of the Holocaust going on in Europe. Political violence echoes the personal violence building between the two men.

In its pattern of small details, also, the book returns to and recomposes its motifs.

Look at their occupations. Darryl is an archeologist opening up the earth. When he thinks of the wife who left him, from whom he was aloof, he understands her only by looking at the things she has left on her dresser: a hair brush, a mirror, objects he examines as if they were pieces of an ancient excavation.

He's awkward with Anna, but when he uncovers the first skeleton of a murdered woman (the sexing of a skeleton is a matter of feeling the pelvis; certain parts of the pelvis gape open farther in a woman), this is an intensely erotic scene. The young woman's presence in his consciousness is very strong.

On the second page of the book, he pauses and wipes his brow. He looks at the trowel in his hand, his primary tool for uncovering the past, and he notes that the blade is as strong and as flexible "as a Toledo sword." Toledo, Spain, was a great sword-making center at the time that these Indians he's uncovering flourished.

Well into the book, 158 pages into it, one of the ranchers who has been displaced by the government comes and takes Darryl and his two grad assistants hostage. The army has the place surrounded. The rancher threatens to kill his hostages. At some point, the young woman starts to weep, which angers the rancher, and he moves his rifle as if to kill her. Darryl is appalled, but what can he do? The rancher doesn't kill her, but a few moments later, to show he means business, he turns and fires his gun, and what he chooses for a target is the skull of one of the young women. The skull shatters. This is what makes Darryl act and exposes the pattern of his psychology. Lying there unnoticed in the dirt is the trowel that was introduced a hundred pages earlier in what metaphor? The Toledo sword. That's what he uses to kill the rancher. He is capable of killing a man, and he does it with what is the very symbol of his humane science but which was introduced with a metaphor of violence.

Lloyd will eventually come to rape Anna Brown. But let me tell you first about that atomic bomb and Lloyd's work. The first atom bomb was a fusion device, which means that in the middle of the bomb is a bit of fissionable plutonium to start the chain reaction. Around it are packed conventional explosives, and then surrounding all of that a lens (and it requires a very precise development to get it just the right shape). When the explosives are set off, the shock wave travels outward, but instead of dispersing outward, it hits the lens and is redirected with exponentially greater force into the center—that is, into the plutonium. And that force is sufficient to start the chain reaction.

Early in the book, Lloyd meditates on the bomb he is creating, and how in his own mind does he see this fusion process? He says, "The plutonium waits in the center of the bomb like a bride."

Well, the fusion process is exactly the process of Lloyd's psychology. He's a man of the mind, rigorously so. He keeps the explosive potential of his violence within him. He proposes to Anna—he wants to make her his *bride*—and she turns him down pretty sharply. It's the way he shuts in—ignores— his explosive rage that eventually leads him to rape her. The rape scene, which is very near the end of the book, though it is an in-the-moment, through-the-senses scene, is also a pre- cise metaphor for the bomb Lloyd has created. It waits in the center like a bride.

You understand what I'm saying now, in this artificial way, with regard to this one novel, about the sensual pattern- ing of details. The bomb, the fusion process, the abusive fa- ther, the trowel, the sword, the bride, the ancient murders, the hostage-taking rancher, the rape, the Holocaust, the uncov- ering of the past, and the containing of violence: event ech- oes detail, sensual moment becomes metaphor, returning, recomposing, and reincorporating toward the phenomena of resonance and motif.

PART TWO

THE WORKSHOP

6

READING, LIT CRIT, AND THE WORKSHOP

"Aesthetics is for artists as ornithology is for the birds."
—Barnett Newman

Don't underestimate the powers inside you that would have you flinch and convince you that you are doing the right thing.

Here's a good one. *Let's read a good book. Let's read the latest Janet Burroway novel.* Now, of course you must read in order to be a writer, and read ravenously. But there are points in your writing day, and even in your life, when you run the danger of hiding in somebody else's voice, somebody's else's vision and sensibility. A moment comes when it's time to find your own artistic identity and find a way into your unconscious. And then you will need to manage your reading carefully. There are even wonderful ideas that another voice will give you, which seem to be furthering your writing career but in fact may be invitations to avert your eyes. You have to write.

Readers as well as writers need to understand that if a work of art is not an object of the mind, if a work of art is a product of the dreamspace, then a reader's primary encounter with this object also needs to be in the dreamspace. As I mentioned earlier, as readers you need primarily and necessarily to *thrum* to the work.

When I say that, I know I put myself in the position of contradicting much of what you've learned about how to read. So be it—because I think that some very basic mistakes have been made in how you have been taught to read. The pedagogical approach itself may not be inappropriate, but there are important caveats that need to attend it in order for you to make sense of the process.

Walker Percy made a wonderful point about the semiotics of the novel: he thinks that a novel, for all its length, is just an extremely long name for a complex, evolving emotion that has no name but that. I've often thought that if someone were to ask me what's the meaning of my novel *Fair Warning*, the only answer is: read it again. *Fair Warning* is a 75,000-word name for a complex, evolving emotion or state of being or state of the universe—and, therefore, even what it's the name *of* is not statable. The Maori of New Zealand have a name for a hill that translates as "The Place Where Tomatia, the Man with Big Knees, Who Slid, Climbed, and Swallowed Mountains, Known As Land-Eater, Played on the Flute to His Loved One." And that's rather like a novel. What's the name of that mountain? Well, it's this. To ask, *What does that name mean?* is meaningless. It has no other meaning; the name is irreducible. So too are the novel and the short story, irreducible names.

Your experience of this name should be *aesthetic*, not analytical. A kind of harmonic resonance is set up within you. That is the primary and appropriate response to a work of art.

You don't listen to a Beethoven symphony or look at a Monet painting or watch Suzanne Farrell dance and walk away with your head full of ideas, having, say, sat in your chair and had the keen intellectual enjoyment of watching the way the themes of the first movement were echoed in the second and then turned into that crescendo in the fourth. That's a separate kind of pleasure with certain value, but it is not the aesthetic response.

It seems to me that a lot of literature classes go wrong because the teachers, unintentionally but often intentionally, give the impression that writers are rather like idiots savants: they really want to say abstract, theoretical, philosophical things, but somehow they can't quite make themselves do it. So they create these objects whose ultimate meaning and relevance and value come into being only after they have been subjected to the analysis of thoughtful literary critics, who translate that work into theoretical, philosophical, ideational terms. And that is somehow the final usefulness, purpose, and meaning of the work. In how many literature classes have you heard it asked, "What does this work mean?" As if it had no meaning in the mere reading of it. Or, worse, "What is the author trying to say?" Trying. You've been in the presence of these attitudes, have you not? Well, this is nonsense, folks. Absolute nonsense. In the presence of such attitudes, your ability to read a work of literary art is actually being destroyed. I suspect the reason cinema is presently the most popular art form in our culture is that so few people have had film appreciation classes. They still are capable of an aesthetic response in a movie house.

But, ironically, I think that many of those literature classes could be taught exactly the same way and be beneficial if two things were said, which everybody then understood and believed. Every literature course in the country should begin with this announcement: *What we're going to do this semester is a purely secondary and artificial thing. We are going to do that in order to tune up the instrument inside you which thrums. We're going to add some new strings in the upper and lower registers. We're going to tune up all the strings, so that after you've taken the course, when you encounter a work of art, you will thrum to it more harmoniously and completely.*

Then it's OK, teach the same things that are taught.

The last thing that needs to be said in every literature course in the country is this: *Now that we have done this artificial and secondary thing in order to tune up your instrument, your final assignment is: forget everything we've said. Because if you don't forget it, when you encounter your next work of art, if you begin to translate it into terms of ideas and theory, breaking it into its parts even as you read—then I have destroyed your ability to have an aesthetic response and to encounter a work of art in the way it was intended. I have taught you how to miss the essence of this object.*

If you take literature courses and these things are not said, then please fill in those blanks. Give yourself that warning at the beginning of the course and that final assignment at the end.

Let me say that what I stress here, what I obsess about, I think is absolutely crucial to assimilate into your artistic process. There may seem to be resident in that obsession a criticism of the way others teach this subject. That criticism is not intended and would be wrong. I think you absolutely need to hear the things that I obsess about, since they are the foundations for other insights—you need, for example, to get to the matters of craft and technique once you have earned that step by getting your process right. But do not infer any criticism of anybody's else's workshop here at FSU. We are a bunch of obsessives, each in our cage, and you slip into the cage and crouch in a corner. It is necessary for you to slip into several of our cages, because my obsessions are different from Mark's, are different from Elizabeth's, are different from Virgil's—you need exposure to all of us. The nice thing about it is that we're a complementary group of writing teachers. If I were your only teacher, something would be missing for you. So it's really important for you to be exposed to all of us or many of us. *Let a hundred flowers bloom*, as Chairman Mao once said.

Also, please understand that you're in a terrific school, because the literature people in this English department actually love and appreciate literature. This is not always the case. There are graduate English programs in this country where no literature is taught at all—only secondary sources, books about the books, are taught—literally. There are a lot of wonderful literature teachers here at this university and almost none of the syndrome that I was describing to you. So it's good you are required to take literature courses. You're in a good place.

Now, let's talk about the workshop, how we'll run a workshop with the insights I've been trying to give you. I offer this to you as a model if you choose to teach with the same emphasis I have or even as a model for informal writing groups. All writing workshops have a built-in danger. If you are in the place in your creative development where you really need to get in touch with your unconscious—the point where my particular obsession is what you need the most—there are certain aspects of common pedagogy that need to be drastically adjusted. One of them is your pace of production. None of you will have an externally fixed quota of words placed upon you this semester. It's a kind of honor system. You need to start meditating every day, and if you're not writing you should at least be going into your trance to free-float, free-associate. At some point you will need to be writing, and then—I've already told you that you have to write every day.

A few weeks into the course you need to catch me and we'll set up a personal goal for you—where you feel you are in terms of your unconscious, what you think would be a reasonable production for the semester. The point of this class is to get you out of your heads, so I don't want to put you under strictures of production that will force you to start willing things into being. You do not have to workshop at all this semester, any given one of you. If on a particular week, no one has anything to workshop, that's OK. We'll come, we'll meet, we'll talk, meditate or whatever, and you'll go away.

If you have a novel to write, and the system I taught you last week is really tapping into your unconscious, then after most of the semester is spent dreamstorming and working up your possible scenes, we might want to make your goal just the first few pages of your novel, which you could give me at the end of the semester. Be very flexible in terms of your production goals.

The workshop is open to fragments, but they need to be the opening fragments of the work. I'm not going to be dogmatic about how a particular piece manifests from your unconscious. I have some suggestions, but there's some wiggle room there. As I indicated to you, my use of that system of predreaming changed with virtually every book. But I do think doing a fair amount of writing ahead of sequence is fraught with dangers. For inexperienced writers, it's usually a way of avoiding the hard stuff. So if you're going to bring a partial something in, let it be the beginning, and please make sure we all understand that's what it is when you hand it in.

We can effectively do probably four manuscripts a week, and if they're fragments, probably more. So, theoretically, we've got enough spots that everybody can submit twice. If one person wants to submit six pieces, that's fine, because I'm sure there are some who'll prefer not to workshop at all. I've never had a class where somebody who wanted to workshop didn't have the chance. If you put in a fragment early on, it's not as if you then go to the back of the line. If you don't workshop at all, then we'll have a one-on-one meeting at the end of term.

Another thing that will be different from other workshops is that you are not required to say anything about anybody else's work. You will have the opportunity to, but there is no requirement. I want to help prevent you from reading from your head. When you get your fellow student's manuscript, you must read it as a work of art. You probably shouldn't have a pen in your hand. You certainly should not be asking yourself, "What am I going to say?" Not even if it's from a benign impulse—and it usually is. Certainly not, "I'm going to get this son of a bitch because he got me last week," and especially not, "Butler's my way into publishing and not only am I going to have a chance to impress him with my work, I'm going to impress everyone with my critical acumen and my eloquence about matters aesthetic." I am not impressed that way. It will not affect your grade. I don't give a damn if you ever write a brilliant book review. But if such things are in your consciousness, the chances of your reading a manuscript the way it's intended to be read are very slim. That's why when you read that work, the first time through especially, it's just as if it's been written by Leo Tolstoy or Flannery O'Connor. You read it as a work of art, and you go *thrum thrum thrum*, and then perhaps you hit a *twang*. The second time through you have a pen handy: *thrum thrum thrum, twang*; you mark the passage and you keep thrumming on or twanging on.

When you go back and examine the twang, I want you to focus not on the symptoms—that is, the technical aspects of it—but the cause. Think of cause in light of what I've been saying about process. If the evidence shows that this work absolutely comes from the unconscious and the character has manifest, felt yearning, only then can you begin to think in technical terms. I don't want to hear technical observations until these other things are right. My most common critique will be to show you in the text where I feel the yearning is absent; the indicators that the fiction came from your head.

I warn you that my most common recommendation will be: *Put this away and never look at it again. Do not rewrite, do not edit, do not fiddle, do not work this over. It came from the wrong place. You see how you got into your head this time; next time go somewhere else.* In your own criticism of each other, as well, I want you to focus on the root problems—yearning, moment-to-moment sensual experience—we've been talking about here. Then we can move on to matters of craft and technique that you'll get with brilliant insight elsewhere.

In our workshops, always cite text when you comment. *This is the spot.* And if you can't say what the matter is exactly, don't make something up. Just say, "You know, I don't know why this didn't work but it didn't work for me here," and we can examine it. Don't feel we've got to find technical solutions or think up reasons. That draws you into your head too, and I'd rather you say, "Fourth paragraph, twang," and that's your critical comment, and that will be useful.

Misty has asked about a problem beyond the workshop. She says she's got stories that she's worked on for two or three years. These stories were workshopped, and she got a lot of suggestions, and she did a lot of revising, and yet there's so much work to be done—there always seems to be work to be done—that she doesn't even feel she should send them out. What do you do? How do you know when to send a story out and when to give up on it? Well, any short story you've been working on for two or three years—this might not be true of a novel, of course—the odds are that the story came from your head to start with. You need to go back and look at it as if you were a reader coming to somebody else's work. If you are convinced that in spite of all the problems in that story, the work originated in your unconscious, and you feel there is manifest yearning in that character, then by all means you should revisit it. But just as you can have bad from-the-head writing, you can have bad from-the-head criticism, so I would urge you to go back to the very first draft you did and put aside anything anybody has said to you. Go back to the draft that is closest to your center. It may need work—even if we are in touch with our unconscious, parts of the story get willed in and some don't, so you still have to overcome all that—but the fact is that many, many workshops give wrongheaded criticism. You know, it's the blind leading the potentially sighted here. And ultimately, you will and should have only a very small number of people you trust to read your work.

So revisit your own work as if it were someone else's; do the best you can with it, and when you've revisited it a few times, and the twangs are now essentially gone in your own artistic view, put it in an envelope and send it out. As soon as you put it out in the world, let it go; just let it go. You move on to the next thing kicking around in your unconscious; you go down there and wrestle it out of there. Just keep on doing that.

If somebody rejects the story, with whatever criticism— you're going to get bad criticism from literary magazines too, let's face it—you let it go. What is the editorial reader's frame of mind? They have fifty things on their desk today, and there are going to be fifty tomorrow, and the next day, and the next. Do you think this puts them in a frame of mind where they are naked to each manuscript they open? Where they put aside the worldview they've held all their lives and open up to a new voice, a new vision of the world? Rarely. That's why a lot of bad stuff gets perpetuated, the bland stuff and the mediocre stuff. It's because often those screening readers—I'm talking about those first two people who see it—those readers, just by the very nature of what they do, are going to be if not consciously looking for, at least more open to, things familiar to them. So all of this works against the unique voice of the real artist. And this happens at the highest, most prestigious, slickest magazines—for any number of reasons that don't have to do with art.

This is a good moment to make another point about how to read a work of art. You should read slowly. You should never read a work of literary art faster than would allow you to hear the narrative voice in your head. Speed-reading is one reason editors and, not incidentally, book reviewers can be so utterly wrongheaded about a particular work of art. By their professions they are driven to speed-read. Some book reviewers review three or four books a week. Such reviewers could theoretically be fine on works of nonfiction. Or certain works of fiction that do not rely on many of the essential qualities I've been trying to identify for you as the characteristics of art. But if you read four books a week and you read them all at pretty much the same pace, you are inevitably going to be a bad reader of literature. A speed-reader necessarily reads for concept, skipping "unnecessary" words; she is impervious to the rhythms of the prose and the revelations of narrative voice and the nuances of motif and irony. This makes a legitimate response to a work of art impossible.

For this and for other nonaesthetic reasons, you're going to get all kinds of responses from all kinds of people in your lives, folks, and the nonsense never ends. It will never end for you, so you need to cultivate *now* your own inner confidence in your vision of things.

Of course, the flip side of that is I had such inner confidence when I wrote "The Chiêu Hồi," the terrible story I'm going to read to you next week, that I was blind to its deficiencies. It's a paradox of life as an artist (or an artist manqué).

While I'm at it, let me make a point about life experience. You grew up reading novels and collections of short stories—or Janet and I did—where no matter how short the bio of the eminent writer, there'd be a sentence like, "He picked grapes in California, drove an ambulance in Italy, worked as a newspaper reporter. Dishwasher. Worked in a power plant in Mississippi"—and so forth. It was understood in the culture that artists had to be directly connected to the real world. Now, even in this day and age, people who get lost in the track I'm about to describe to you have some kind of childhood or young adulthood, and the first novel of the hot young writer with the big-name publisher takes its power from the fact that there was some life actually lived at some point. But the bio says, "Got his undergraduate degree at Amherst or Brown, took his MFA at the University of Iowa, and has been teaching at such and such a college." The second novel, if the author is lucky, is a kind of derivation of the first; but the third novel is about a professor having an affair with a student, and the fourth novel is about a novelist. You just see the life—and, not incidentally, the career—shutting down. Then this author starts writing nonfiction. The enduring artists are ravenous for life, ravenous for experience. And so the things you've done in the world beyond academia, things that are not rooted in books and defined by ideas, these things fill up your unconscious, they are the primary stuff of your compost heap.

Now, in the context of certain stories or books you are given to write, some of your "life experience" will necessarily have to come from a kind of research, and I'd like to mention several rich resources for that research—beginning with the Internet, which is a whole new sort of library for writers. The kinds of sense detail you need are available in a way that they never were before. An example from my own experience: in *Mr. Spaceman* there's an old woman telling a story about her youth when she went out walking, came over the peak of a sand dune, and observed the flight of the first Wright brothers plane—which gave her the lifelong yearning to fly. When she describes that plane later in her life, she would know exactly what kind of cloth was stretched over the skeleton. But I didn't know. Now, how do you find out such a detail? You could spend hours searching in a traditional library—because you wouldn't find it in the obvious places like an encyclopedia. But on the Internet—at the time, Google didn't exist; AltaVista was the best search engine, so I went to AltaVista and put in "Wright brothers," "plane," and "material," and "cloth." Three minutes later, I'm at a Smithsonian Institute Web page where I discover that it was muslin.

There are also a number of useful books that should be on your shelf. One that's really helpful in terms of sense details is called *The Oxford-Duden Pictorial English Dictionary*, published by Oxford University Press. It's about 650 pages of line drawings of everything under the sun—a warehouse, a riverfront, a grocery store, whatever, and each of these very detailed drawings has sixty or seventy little numbered arrows to tell you what every part is called. If your character is walking out onto a pier in the Hudson River, and you have him sit down on one of those tubular, rounded things that comes out of the pier, with ropes around it where they tie up the ship— you sort of lose the moment if you say, "Well, he sat down on that tubular thing. . . ." OK, you go to the drawing of the docks and you see an arrow pointing at that thing and, by golly, it's a *bollard*. They've got two pages of hats that tell you the difference between a porkpie and a boater and a bowler and a fedora, and so forth. It's a great resource.

The *Merriam-Webster's Collegiate* and the *Random House Webster's Unabridged* are to my knowledge the only two dictionaries of American English that will tell you when a word entered the language—and when you're writing in period that can be crucial to know. I was writing *Wabash*, set in 1932, and the cop was swinging—I was going to say a *billy club*, but *billy club* came into the language in the 1940s. *Nightstick* came in at the turn of the twentieth century, so it's his nightstick he's swinging, not his billy club. These are very useful dictionaries in that respect. And, of course, there is the venerable *Oxford English Dictionary*, that gives you the timing for every subdefinition of each word, which the other two do not.

Another useful book is *The Pantone Book of Color* by Leatrice Eiseman and Lawrence Herbert, published by the art house Harry Abrams, which contains thousands of different shades of colors along with their official names. Sometimes having such a visual point of reference will be helpful.

There are several books that can aid you with period detail, but one I like is called *American Costume, 1915–1970* by Shirley Miles O'Donnol, Indiana University Press, which will show you what people wore every day. You might also look for copies of all those wonderful old reproductions of Sears, Roebuck catalogs, which were popular a few years ago. You should steal a big city phone book next time you go to New York or Los Angeles.

There are a number of baby-naming books that I find really useful. One I especially like is *Beyond Jennifer and Jason, Madison and Montana*, which gives the period popularity, connotation, classical meaning, and so forth of hundreds of names. I find it useful to name my characters very early in the process, and it can be important to find the right name.

There's a great book called *A Field Guide to American Houses*, which will give you a view of and the accurate names for architectural features of common domiciles. Another, called *American Shelter*, is also useful in this regard.

It's a good idea to have handy a good slang dictionary. Two I recommend are *The New Dictionary of American Slang* and the *Thesaurus of American Slang*, both edited by Robert Chapman.

7

THE BAD STORY

"The novel is a pack of lies hounding the truth."
—Carlos Fuentes

I know that you've read "Open Arms" for tonight [see appendix], which is a story I'm proud of. But if I'm going to critique many of your stories by telling you to put them away and never look at them again, I think it's only fair that I begin by exposing to you a story that I had to put away and never look at again—except for the purpose of illustrating a good writer's bad beginnings—a story whose origins were, eventually, eighteen years later, recomposted into "Open Arms."

So tonight I'm going to treat you to that awful story, and I'm going to begin by reading a bit from the notebook that I carried around Vietnam in my hip pocket. I carried it with great self-importance. My ambition back then was to be famous. I carried that book in my hip pocket thinking that I could see it under glass some day: *This was the curve of his butt. These are the smudges made by his fingers. Yes, this was his toothbrush.*

These are the false things, where ambition goes wrong.

Your ambition as an artist is to give voice to the deep, inchoate vision of the world that resides dynamically in your unconscious. That's what you must keep focused on; that's the only ambition worth anything to you as an artist. The desire to give voice and the desire to be published sometimes feel like the same thing, but they're not. The dream that comes from your white-hot center and the dream of fame—they are not the same.

In any case, I always carried a notebook around and I made hundreds of notes. After I figured out what art is all about, I never looked back at them again—except to look for this passage; and I didn't do that until I started to teach. Here's the passage from the notebook:

> Núi Đất [the place where I was], *chiêu hồi* [a Viet-
> namese phrase which means essentially "open arms"]
> at the stag films. Former political officer of large crack
> Viet Cong unit now watching the Aussies' Sunday
> night stag films, all four hours of them. Communist
> intense prudishness: punish people for having a pinup;
> what does he think of this? I talk to him later. He is
> very intelligent. A VC adjutant went to hills because
> he hated the wasteful, inefficient, corrupt government,
> and also because one day his wife and child were stand-
> ing in a doorway and an ARVN [Army of the Repub-
> lic of Vietnam; that is, South Vietnamese] soldier
> gunned them down. Went to the hills. Finally decided
> that the war would never end this way, returned and

became bushman scout for the Aussies, took them to base camp after base camp. Names, stats on dozens of VCI [Viet Cong infrastructure, the shadow government people]. Driving through village, saw woman, just lower half of face, identified her as VCI. He met her only once six weeks ago. It took him four days to find the ARVN soldier before he went to the hills. The *chiêu hôi* was a platoon leader of Sapper Recon Platoon. Went to COSVN, which is the North Vietnamese Army headquarters that nobody ever found. Went to Cambodia, a month's march. There he learned sapper techniques. One day I was watching Vietnamese television. He came in and smiled and he sat down with me. He asked if I spoke Vietnamese. He asked if I was an American. We talked and watched television together. I told him what I thought of the Vietnamese people, their warmth and kindness to me in spite of the bitterness they should have after all these years of the war. He said they'd had hundreds of years of war already—the Chinese, the French, and so forth—and it is part of life. He said they all want peace very badly, both those who speak against the war and those who make the war, but when the Americans and Australians pull out the Communists will take over. He says the Communists don't allow people to be anything but poor, don't allow people to print newspapers or speak against the government. The people who are against the war don't understand this; he says when you have a choice between a bad Communist government and a bad democratic government, you must choose the

bad democratic government because you can change it
eventually.

That's what was in this little notebook I carried around.
About six months after that event, I wrote the first short story
I ever wrote as an adult. I had finally decided that I wasn't
going to write plays; my future was in fiction. Luckily I didn't
know how far-off that future was. The story is called "The
Chiêu Hôì," and—I take a deep breath—here it is:

"Hey, Yank! You sure you want to stay around? We've
got some bloody hot stag films coming up." The warrant
officer they called Wally laughed and began moving
wicker chairs at the back of the club.
    I hesitated a moment at the half seriousness of his
jibe and thought of the tiny, sweet-smelling, whining girls
lingering in the dark of our company street at Long Binh.
    "Think I'll chance it," I said.
    The snap of canvas in the twilight and I looked
out the big tent at the blowing trees. I'd trade the Aussies
some of our real sex for a few of their trees.
    "You don't get anything like these at your camp."
    "No."
    I heard the crunching of the gravel floor as he
struggled with the chairs. One more look at the trees
going purple outside.
    "Want some help?"
    "You just relax yourself. I can handle these."
    I got up. "I insist."

I went back to him and helped put the chairs in line facing the raised platform at the far end of the club.

"You going to be the projectionist?"

"Yes indeed. It won't be anything fancy, mind you. But the machine's good and we use a nice fresh bedsheet for the screen. Appropriate."

As we laughed, Thanh came in. I had seen him around the camp. One of the very few Vietnamese on the post. He smiled the eager, head-bobbing smile used for foreigners who don't speak Vietnamese and he sat down in a chair near the platform.

"That's Thanh."

"I've seen him around," I said.

"He's a *chieu hoi*. He was the leader of a VC sapper platoon." The Australian paused for effect. I looked at the slim young man quietly smoking a cigarette. There is always a silent moment of shared respect when two allied fighting men talk about sappers. They are the combat engineers who penetrate perimeters and are the toughest, gutsiest VC of all. "If all their blokes were like Thanh, the VC would have kicked our asses into the sea years ago. He's a bushman scout for us now. That little bastard has led us to base camp after base camp. He sat down and wrote out biographies on dozens of VC infrastructure people all over Phuc Tuy province. Incredible mind, that bloke."

Thanh continued smoking, seemingly unaware of our talk. He looked very small, sitting motionless in the large wicker chair.

"Why did he join the VC?"

"In '67 his wife and child were standing in the door of his house. A government soldier gunned them down. Killed them. It took Thanh four days to find the soldier. Then he went to the hills."

I left the Australian and walked forward to where Thanh was sitting. He looked up as I approached and he smiled and nodded again.

"How are you?" he asked slowly in articulated English.

"*Tôi mạnh giỏi. Còn ông thì sao,*" I said. It was the standard Vietnamese reply.

Thanh laughed loud and long and thrust his hand to me. "You speak Vietnamese very well," he said in his own language.

I sat beside him as I shook his hand. "Don't put me on a paper airplane," I said, using the Vietnamese saying that amiably rejects flattery. Thanh laughed loud again.

"Very good. Very good. You are an American, aren't you?"

"Yes. I'm just working with the Australians for a couple of weeks. We exchange people sometimes."

"How long have you been in Vietnam?"

"About three months," I replied.

"And you speak so well? That is amazing."

"I studied for a year in America before I came to Vietnam."

"I see. But you still speak very excellent Vietnamese. It is not the same just to study it. You are very good."

"Thank you. I am happy to have the opportunity
to talk to the Vietnamese people." I began to feel that
inevitable awkwardness that always comes at the start
of conversations, as I sound for many minutes like a daily
dialog from our language textbook.

Thanh took a long puff on his cigarette, savoring
it, and blowing the smoke through his nose. After a
moment of contemplating the cigarette in his hand, he
looked at me and smiled easily again. "What do you
think of Vietnam?"

"I like Vietnam very much," I said. I glanced past
Thanh and out at the darkening sky. "The evenings are
very cool."

"Yes, they are. Very fresh." I looked back at
Thanh. He smiled and nodded, waiting for me to say
more. I looked at his hands. I had heard so many whistles
of respect for sappers from even the most grizzled "gook-
killer" sergeants that I had an almost childish awe of
these small brown hands. The left lay in repose on the
arm of the chair. The right continually rolled the cigarette, meticulously keeping the lit end free of flaking ash.

"The fresh nights are fine to be with someone,"
Thanh said.

I looked up at him. The humor of the statement
startled me as I saw in my mind the night roaming VC
platoons. I could not tell if Thanh intended the joke.

"But is that your only feeling for Vietnam in three months?" he continued.

"No. Of course not."

"I am interested in your feelings."

It seemed a good chance to crawl out of my text-book. "Before I came to Vietnam I had expected half the people to be so miserable from the war that they would hate any foreigner and the other half of the people to be Communist sympathizers and therefore want to kill me."

Thanh laughed.

"But since I have been here I have talked to many Vietnamese people. And it is amazing. Without exception, every man and woman has been as friendly and open as anyone I have ever met."

"Of course."

"In spite of all the years of misery, the Vietnamese people have an innate sense of cheerfulness that is truly extraordinary."

"Vietnamese know how to enjoy life." Now Thanh looked out of the tent. His cigarette was gone and both his hands rested lightly on the arms of the chair. He turned back to me and smiled a more solemn smile. "The Vietnamese have had hundreds of years of war. Many countries have come here to war—China, Cambodia, Japan, France."

"The U.S.," I said.

"Many countries. So the Vietnamese people know what war is. But it makes no difference. If a people know how to enjoy life and they are used to war, it makes no difference. Their life goes on. The war is part of it. But they enjoy living. They are still happy in their days."

Among the high branches a few stars were beginning to appear. Thanh was watching the night now too.

"Why did you join?"

Thanh turned to me. The easy smile was gone. But his solemnity was simply thoughtful, still friendly. After a moment he said, "The government was robbing the people. It was corrupt and wasteful and repressive. At the time, the Communists seemed to offer an alternative." He paused, watching my face closely. I nodded my head and waited for him to say more.

Then I said, "Was that all?"

"No. Of course not." We looked at each other silently for a moment more. Then he said, "They murdered my wife and child." Another pause. "We had only two years together."

Other people were coming in. They were laughing at the back of the club, calling out orders for beer, pulling chairs around.

"And why did you leave the VC?"

"'The purity of the revolution must be preserved. The corruptions of the body are part of the decadence of our enemies.' One of the men in another platoon was caught making love to one of the nurses and was shot." Thanh thought a moment and then added, "Of course, that was logical to them."

People were sitting just behind us now. Talking loudly and sitting on my other side now too. Thanh paused and I leaned closer.

"The Communists love no one. They love nothing," he said.

The OC made a little speech about keeping the noise down but how it was difficult to applaud with one hand anyway and everyone laughed and the lights went out and the films began. There were nine twenty-minute Danish films. Three hours of close-ups. Working bodies. And hands. Avid hands.

Thanh sat unmoving through all nine films. He watched and the three-hour string of male jokes at the screen must have been nothing but a blur of foreign words. He watched earnestly, his hands quiet.

When the lights came up, Thanh and I remained as the others drifted out of the tent or back to the bar. Thanh was looking at his hands.

"Enjoyable, wasn't it?" I said.

"It was so short."

At first I didn't understand. Three hours, after all. I smiled.

"Only two years." He looked at me. Then the easy smile came again. He shook my hand and we spoke the conventional Vietnames good-byes before he left.

Lots of stuff wrong with this; in fact, everything's wrong with it in exactly the way I've been describing. "Hey, Yank . . ." Opening with a piece of dialogue very rarely works, because there's no context. And, important, in this whole piece there's not a single line of dialogue with *subtext*. Nothing's going on beneath the surface. Dialogue gives you the illusion of moment-to-moment sensual experience—after all, these are the words this character is speaking aloud in the moment—but in bad dialogue all you're getting is the information, exposition, or emotional declaration; and that's where your summary, your generalization, your abstraction, your analysis, run and hide in plain sight. Beware of that as you work to get that unselected, unironic, there-for-information stuff out of your writing: it's going to try to find a new home in the mouths of your characters. This story is full of sheer chunks of analysis and abstraction, often straight from my undigested notes, included just for the convenience of the story.

The story is also inorganic. Even though there appears to be a motif, the images are totally unrelated. *Looking out of the tent,* and *the trees,* and *going purple against the sky*—what's all that about? It does not connect in its sensual pattern to anything going on in the story. Remember that I had written twelve just as awful plays, so these passages are like little stage directions (which was my failure as a playwright too): *He's looking, I'm looking out, then he looks out, and I look out, and now we're both looking out.* No resonance whatsoever.

The trap of literal memory is very clear here. It was eighteen years later that I wrote "Open Arms," which as you can see grew out of the composting of the same event. Let's call "The Chiêu Hôì" the bad story and "Open Arms" the good story. In the bad story, things happen exactly as they did in real life, whereas the good story involves a dramatic inversion of the literal event. In the bad story Thanh's motivation is that he was in a place where he was comfortable and where he belonged, a South Vietnamese democratic society. The thing he did against his own deeper nature was go off to join the VC in response to the killing of his wife and child by a South Vietnamese soldier. And now, in the bad story, he's basically back where he belongs. You notice that in "Open Arms" all this is inverted. He was a Viet Cong true believer and the Viet Cong killed his wife and child, and this Australian porn show where we find him is not where he belongs but a place where he *also* doesn't belong. I had to free myself from the way it literally happened in order to make "Open Arms" work.

In the bad story the narrator is a passive observer. It's me. I'm sure every one of you has at least one story—and you may write another—where you are the sensitive writer responding to this unusual character you've met in life. You encounter somebody interesting and you go, *Oh boy, that's a story.* You sit down and write it, putting yourself in the middle as a passive observer watching this other person. Right? What's missing in every story where you've got a passive observer in the middle? The yearning. If the narrator in my bad story desires anything at all, it's to show what a swell sensitive American guy he is. Which of course is not a yearning at all. The narrator is doing fine, meeting this interesting guy he can communicate with in his own language, and the guy's doing fine, back where he belongs. Oh yeah, his wife and child are dead, but, you know, that's a problem, not a yearning. The dynamics of desire are utterly missing.

I don't care how smart you are. Your mind is stupid artistically, and here's another striking example of that. I have to emphasize that this event in the story I'm about to point out *did not happen* in real life. In "The Chiêu Hồi," this sensitive American who speaks Vietnamese says, "Why did you join?" Thanh turns to him. His "easy smile was gone. . . ." And Thanh even tries to avoid answering. " 'The government was robbing the people. It was corrupt and wasteful and repressive . . .'" And so forth. Then Thanh pauses, obviously hoping that's all he has to say on the subject. And the narrator drills in. " 'Was that all?'" he asks. He *makes* Thanh talk about the tragedy.

This is utterly cruel. But it's no longer about people, it's about crudely applying fiction technique. The writer wants to get this information about Thanh into the story in his own voice, and to show how the guy is struggling, trying not to face the terrible thing that's happened. Gee, how do you show that? Well, you have your narrator ask him, and when he waffles, you press him. Now I promise you I never would have done this in real life. But when I wrote the story I was totally oblivious to the moral implications and didn't notice until I came to teach creative writing and pulled the old bad story out that this sensitive American guy does something truly heinous. That's what comes from writing from your head. As writers we must have compassion for all the characters we create. If we're going to play God, we have to be a loving God, and you can't love with your brain.

By contrast, the Vietnamese narrator in "Open Arms," whose yearning resonates organically into the story as it's reconceived, does a similar heinous thing; but he himself is conscious of it—and so am I as writer. Both the Vietnamese narrator in "Open Arms" and the American narrator in "Chiêu Hôi" know ahead of time that the man's family was murdered and that is why he left his home. In both cases, even though they know it, they make him say it. But the Vietnamese narrator, says: "To my shame." He says it both times. *To my shame.* He knows he's doing a terrible thing here and acknowledges it. We see that tension in him.

Of course, you might write a story with an insensitive character like the narrator of "The Chiêu Hôi." Obviously there are cruel characters and cruel acts in fiction. But in that story the cruelty is totally incidental—or maybe the intent of the author was to show a sensitive guy responding to a sad character who misses his wife. And that's all he takes away from an afternoon of porn films. How pathetic. The narrator's insensitivity is not an issue; there's no repercussion, there's no realization, and no seeming ill effect on Thanh. We don't see the cruelty of it in any manifest way. It's just on-the-surface cruelty, and it stays on the surface.

Let me elaborate on a point I made earlier in passing about the beginning of "Open Arms": "I have no hatred in me. I am almost certain of that." How do you establish dramatic irony in a story? Well, to begin with, anyone who has to say he's got no hatred in him is already protesting too much. And then, one way to suggest irony is with a qualifier, in this case just that one word *almost.* "I have no hatred in me. I am almost certain of that." He has self-doubt that lets us doubt him. "I fought for my country long enough to lose my wife to another man, a cripple. This was because even

though I was alive, I was dead to her, being far away. Perhaps it bothers me a little"—*perhaps*—"that his deformity was
something he was born with and not earned in the war. But
even that doesn't matter. In the end, my country itself was
lost. . . ." *My country*.

This whole story, as you soon learn, has to do with trying to find a place in the world. "In the end my country was
lost and I am no longer there. . . ." It's not that it's no longer
his country, it *is* his country, but he's no longer there. He takes
some pleasure in the fact that his wife and her new lover are
suffering. And then he brings up this stranger, this guy:

> . . . who suffered the most complicated feeling I could
> imagine. It is he who makes me feel sometimes that I
> am sitting with my legs crossed in an attitude of peace
> and with an acceptance of all that I've been taught about
> the suffering that comes from desire.

Let me indulge in a bit of artificial and secondary analysis. The Vietnamese narrator asserts that he understands the
story he's going to tell. As a result of it, he has accepted his
fate. None of that's true. I hope you understand the irony at
the end, that little litany of *I'm OK: I've got a VCR, I've got a
good job, there's no hatred in me, everything's fine*. Not so. He is
utterly lost, for the same reason as that other man, Thap, who
came to a moment in which he realized that he had no country whatsoever. That's what our narrator is really responding
to, because in spite of his avowals at the end of the story, deep
down he feels he belongs nowhere. *I live on Mary Poppins Drive*

in Gretna, Louisiana. . . . And of course, his yearning is for a place in the world.

Understand that when I came to write "Open Arms," I did not refer to this older story at all. In 1988 I was finishing my sixth novel, *The Deuce,* which is in the voice of a sixteen-year-old half-Vietnamese, half-American former Saigon street kid who ends up on Forty-second Street in the bad old days before Mickey Mouse overran the place. Alan Cheuse called me to say he was producing a series for National Public Radio called *The Sound of Writing,* and he was soliciting original short stories that would be read by actors on the radio. He said, *Would you give us one? You bet.* I hung up the phone and . . . *what have I done?* I was writing good novels, and I'd convinced myself that it's a rare writer who is adept in both forms. I went back to those stories to see if there was something I could salvage, but they were worse than I remembered. So I put them away again.

However, there was a bit of Vietnamese folkway on one of the three-by-five cards I'd made for *The Deuce,* which I'd expected to put into the novel but hadn't. The card that fell out of the stack had to do with a Vietnamese boy who loved to catch, train, and fight crickets. Suddenly a voice came out of my unconscious, the voice of a Vietnamese father in Lake Charles, Louisiana, on a Sunday afternoon. Everything's boring and dull and his son is bored and he tries to interest the kid in cricket fighting. So I sat down and wrote it in one six-and-a-half-hour stretch. It turned out well.

I went to bed that night and the next morning when I woke up I had two dozen other voices in my unconscious, saying *me, me, me*. All the stories in *A Good Scent from a Strange Mountain* presented themselves to me at once. When "Open Arms" came to me, it was not in reference to that old story; it wasn't even a reference to the notebook. I didn't look at the notebook either. The voices came strictly from my unconscious at that point.

Before you go, let me give you an assignment for next week: you'll need to be able to tell some personal anecdote, something you've told before aloud. I don't want you to give this any thought; you don't need to write it out; it doesn't need to be profound; it can be totally trivial: taking a shower, sitting at a traffic light. You don't have to be funny, it doesn't have to be moving or well told. Just tell an anecdote as you would over coffee. Of course it's going to be full of summary and generalization and analysis. It should be. An anecdote is not a work of art; it's something else. So do the something else. It'll give me a little fragment of your life to walk you back through in a special exercise.

8

THE ANECDOTE EXERCISE

"Man, if you gotta ask, you'll never know."
—*Louis Armstrong, when asked to define jazz*

How many seriously want to do this tonight? We're going to hear your informal anecdotes first, so you have to make a quick choice about whether you're open to doing this in front of the class. You will also get a fair amount of benefit from just observing and listening. Volunteers . . . ?

You have to actually lift your arm above your head. One, two, three, four.

Good. Now the four of you are going to tell your anecdotes as you would over a couple of beers, and after you're all done I'll bring you up front one at a time. Everyone else—these are your instructions for the evening—when we redo these little narratives, nobody look at the speaker. Or at me. All of you are to go into your trance state and participate moment to moment with the person retelling a fragment of the anecdote. You will all stare at a blank sheet of paper, or your thumbs, or you'll close your eyes, meditating. You will concentrate on evoking the images that come out of the subject's mouth. I promise you, we will not get past the barest first few moments of the anecdote.

Those of you in front of the class: I will walk you sentence by sentence through a fragment of your anecdote, demanding absolutely pure moment-to-moment through-the-senses narrative. When you vary from that, I will gently identify the way in which you vary it and have you back up. Then at some point I will even step in and make you consider certain things: *What do you smell?*—and so forth.

At every question, at every little fork in the road for the speaker, I want you at your desks to be making those same decisions. And if your decisions are different from the speaker's, fine; then back up, edit that, and keep going forward. I want you to be participating internally.

We're going to be utterly obsessive about moment-to-moment sensual flow of narrative here. We're not going to do any fast motion or slow motion, we're not going to allow the narrator the leeway of abstraction and generalization and interpretation that are sometimes allowable as voice—none of that tonight. The details that I'm going to be eliciting have no center of gravity to them, because we're not going to get involved with yearning; that will emerge, we hope, next week in the coached writing exercise. But tonight there's no center of gravity, so the details will be promiscuous.

Understand that what's coming out of your mouth is not the same as writing a work of literary fiction. It has a superficial similarity to literary fiction, but the purpose of the exercise is simply to make you understand what the normal mode of literary discourse is, what your normal focus and speed are in literary fiction, and to open up your sense memory and, therefore, to open you up to your unconscious. Don't be disturbed if it's frustrating and nothing comes of it. If you work your way through that, at least you'll feel what's wrong. I've seen spectacular breakthroughs a few times with people doing this exercise, but whatever happens is OK; you won't be graded, no one's judging you. It's just an exercise to help you and your colleagues.

Because I'm going to be asking these questions, and because your literal memories are not sufficient to remember the kinds of detail I'm asking for, I'm obviously not looking for your memories of the actual event. We're using the anecdote as a familiar takeoff point for you, but mostly you're going to be inventing. We're going to lead you to invent a reality for a tiny fragment of the anecdote. So if you don't remember it very well, that's fine too—probably better. The invention must come from your *sense memory*—not your ability to remember exactly where you smelled that thing or exactly what you heard ten years ago; but your ability to collect all the sensual impressions of your life *as impressions*, to break them down in the compost of your imagination, and then to recover them, reevoke them, and recombine them into these new imagined things.

Who's going to go first to tell your anecdote? Sandra—good, thanks.

I'll be taking a few notes, nothing evaluative; I just want to get it down so I'll know where to come back to.

Sandra: I don't remember how old I was, but I walked through the streets of Liverpool to visit my grandfather, who

had a barbershop somewhere. It was probably nearby somewhere, but I thought it was a long way away. And I went to
the shop to visit him, and he was shaving. He used an old-
fashioned razor. He stopped what he was doing—I think he
said something like "Hello luv" to me. And he went over to
the window and he picked up a pair of earrings, which were in
the window. I don't know what he was doing selling earrings,
but they were in the window and he just picked them out and
gave them to me and I put them on. I really loved them. My
wonderful grandfather. My mother never understood why I
liked him when she didn't, but I think that was one of the
crucial moments forming a relationship with him.

ROB: Excellent, that's going to be very useful. That
gives us a lot of good stuff to work with. Who else?

Mary Jane: This is about the day after my father died.
My brother and I drove out to the funeral home to make ar-
rangements for his funeral, and walked in the door, and it was
like a movie cliché of a funeral parlor. It had this really thick
carpeting on the floor and heavy curtains; it was dark inside
and there was air-conditioning and it was really cold. And then
the fellow who was the funeral director—you know, black
mustache and a cheap suit—exactly what you would expect, I
guess. We went in and sat down, my brother and I, across the
table from each other, and went through the checklist of what
you have to do to arrange a funeral. My father wanted to be
cremated, but what we didn't realize is that by law you have
to be cremated in a casket, so we had to choose a casket for
him anyway. So we took a tour of the funeral parlor; we got to
look at all the caskets, and my brother and I decided we would

buy the cheapest thing, which was a cardboard box, which in a way is kind of shameful, but we also looked at each other and thought if we did anything else Dad would kill us if he were here because he wouldn't want to spend the money. Some weird things happened, like we sat there across from each other arranging this funeral, trying not to laugh the day after our father had died, because it was all such a cliché. And I said, "Can I pay for this with a credit card?" and I thought: this is weird, to pay for this with a credit card. And the last thing that happened was somebody had to go and identify the body, and my big, tough, army-helicopter-pilot older brother didn't want to do it, so I did it. I went in and saw my father wrapped up in a blanket, laid out in this room, and somehow I had to touch his head and he was so cold that I thought, "He's been in the refrigerator overnight." It was very strange.

ROB: Thank you, Mary Jane. Brandy?

Brandy: When I was three years old, I went on vacation to Broken Bow, Oklahoma, at Arrowhead State Park, and I was seesawing with both of my brothers, the older brother on one side of me and the next oldest on the other. The middle brother always had middle-child syndrome and couldn't stand me, and he got mad at one point and decided to get off, but he didn't realize that my legs were in the handle part of the seesaw, so when he did, it shot me up in the air and I broke my leg, and I had to drive all the way back home with a broken leg.

ROB: Thank you. That works too. Leslie?

Leslie: When I was small, I grew up in a house surrounded by hay fields and pecan orchards, and in the middle of the fall, about this time of year, my cousin Gaines—who looked a little like Clark Kent, with big bottle glasses—would get on his tractor, and he would mow all the hay and leave hundreds of bales of hay the size of a Volkswagen out on the edge of the pecan orchard. Then my brother and I would climb up on the hay bales and jump from bale to bale and play king of the mountain. The goal was to knock the other person off the bale. When I was very small, I couldn't get onto the hay bales because they were round, and sometimes they'd be so big that I couldn't get a grip in smooth hay without digging into it—and it's hard to dig into it because it's real dense—so I'd have to find two bales that were close together and crawl into that narrow space in between and inch away up sideways, and my brother would knock me off and sometimes it hurt really bad falling down.

ROB: Thank you, Leslie. If the four of you are serious about continuing, then that's probably all we're going to need. Who'd like to go first for the retelling? Come on, Sandra.

All right, I want you to remember that you're all in this together. I want you essentially to take on Sandra's consciousness, participate with her, really try to see this scene—a little bit ahead of her even.

Sandra, I want you to relax, clear your head. Don't consider your words. Speak in full narrative sentences, but don't worry about your grammar and syntax. Just try to keep things flowing, and just let what comes out of your mouth be simply an articulation of what's going on in that cinema of your own mind.

Let's take you from the first moment you step into the barbershop, Sandra. Pick us up there, and understand that the goal is to articulate only in the moment through the senses.

Sandra: I can see a lot of men pushing around me.

ROB: OK, you've just now generalized. "A lot of men" is a generality. You take that first step in the door and you stop. You place yourself in that room and I want you, like the camera eye, to see it in its fullness—look from left to right, up to down, whatever, but let's see what you're seeing in the moment.

Sandra: There are men sitting.

ROB: You've generalized once again. Let's start at one specific spot in the room. If you're taking in a generalized view of the room, it's not really general because, in fact, there's a picture full of detail, but because we're not painters—we're fiction writers—we have to place those details in a sequence, don't we? So take the step in, and I want you to look at a specific spot and see that spot, then move your eyes, and move them, and move them.

Sandra: OK, I go through the door.

ROB: That's also summarized: "I go through the door." There's no engagement of the moment with the doorknob, no sound of the door opening, no feeling of the exchange of air between the outside and barbershop. Do you understand? There are so many moment-to-moment sense impressions going through the door that were left out. What we're looking for is every moment-to-moment detail. But let's not get hung up at the door. You have entered and have just closed the door behind you. You are in your first moment completely in the barbershop. Let your eye fall on one specific thing right now.

Sandra: It's a man.

ROB: Now you've started this with a summarizing statement. I want you to see it in the moment specifically. What is the first feature on that man's whole being? What's the first thing your eyes come to? Engage him with your eyes in the moment. So tell me the first thing you see about that man.

Sandra: I can't see him properly.

ROB: OK, that's probably because you're trying to remember him from the literal event. What I want you to do now is invent him. Make him a sensual reality in this cinema of your mind, in your imagination. Take a moment. You've just touched the brass of that doorknob and it felt cool in the very center of the palm of your hand. You've turned it and you've leaned into the door and it has creaked open and a little bell tinkles at the top and the smell of powder and . . .

Sandra: Shaving cream . . .

ROB: Good. Pick it up. What else comes out of the air as you're just stepping through the door.

Sandra: The sound of the strap as he presses the blade . . .

ROB: OK, the sound of the strap—what is that sound?—give me that sound.

Sandra: Kind of like a dull little whack against the leather strap.

ROB: Good. What else? What else is coming out of you as you're inside.

Sandra: Coughing. Talking.

ROB: OK, you're generalizing those. Let's hear a specific cough, and tell me about that cough. And a fragment of talk. Tell me those things in narrative.

Sandra: A man's coughing.

ROB: Not too much removed from a cough. Tell me about that cough?

Sandra: It's a dry cough.

ROB: From where is it coming?

Sandra: It's coming from his throat.

ROB: All right. Hear a fragment of something that's spoken.

Sandra: I actually hear my grandfather's voice.

ROB: You've just summarized that for me, OK? What is he saying?

Sandra: He's talking about dogs.

ROB: You've summarized what he's talking about. Absolutely drop into the center of the conversation and let me hear a fragment of what he's saying.

Sandra: "Sheila's a beautiful bitch."

ROB: Good, very nice.

Sandra: "Sheila."

ROB: All right. Let your grandfather look in your direction. Tell me what you see and how you see him and what you see him do.

Sandra: He has the razor in his hand.

ROB: That's generalized for me. If that's the sentence, how is he holding it? Give me all the details.

Sandra: He has it pointed out. He's holding his forefinger to the back of the blade, balancing it, holding it very delicately. He's such a big man, he has such a big hand. He's holding the razor very gently and delicately.

ROB: OK, now those are abstractions—gentleness and delicacy. Tell me in the moment through the senses what you are seeing there that you have abstracted as delicate.

Sandra: Lightly. It's a kind of a shape of the hand.

ROB: What shape? How are the fingers arranged?

Sandra: The forefinger's out in front of the blade.

ROB: Where's the pinkie?

Sandra: It's balancing the very end of the razor.

ROB: Let his face turn to you. Let me see his face in the moment.

Sandra: He is not surprised to see me.

ROB: OK, you have just analyzed his face. He's not surprised to see you. We're not seeing a *not-there*; what are we seeing?

Sandra: He's looking as though he was expecting me to walk in.

ROB: You just analyzed it again. What do you read in the face? Because the little girl standing there perhaps rightly analyzes the look on his face, but what is it that's on the face she sees that leads her to that analysis? That's what we're after.

Sandra: That's abstraction?

ROB: That's abstraction. The thwack of that razor on the strop tells me that you have a very fine sense memory and also that you should drop into "She was a beautiful bitch" as the first words out of his mouth. Those are fine, striking moments, Sandra. Now what you need to do is turn that same faculty to this face.

Sandra: He seems to gaze at me with a very level expression. His expression hardly seems to change.

ROB: OK. From what?

Sandra: From what I would have expected him to . . .

ROB: OK, now you're begging the question. What feature on his face are you looking at? Focus on one feature.

Sandra: His eyes.

ROB: Tell me about his eyes.

Sandra: He's gazing.

ROB: Gazing is a kind of generalized thing, isn't it? There is an infinite variety of gazes. What are those eyes? Look at those eyes and let me see precisely what they are.

Sandra: They're blue.

ROB: Blue like what?

Sandra: Actually like a steely kind of blue-gray.

ROB: What do you smell?

Sandra: Tobacco.

ROB: What's that like? There are a lot of different kinds of tobacco. How do you experience that smell?

Sandra: I associate that with men.

ROB: Yeah, that's kind of generalizing for me now. There's a lot of different modulations of tobacco smell and they come to you in various ways. So let me smell that specific tobacco smell.

Sandra: It's sweet. And dark.

ROB: Sweet and dark. That's good. What part of your body does it make you conscious of? Where does it impact your body?

Sandra: In the stomach. It seems to go straight down into me when I smell it.

ROB: Good! OK, thank you Sandra. [Applause and much laughter.] It's very difficult. But so is writing literary fiction. And, you know, you must place these demands on yourself to be in the moment and through the senses. All the time, in everything you write in your fiction, this must be the standard mode of discourse unless and until the organic object not only allows but *demands*, from deep, resonant, dream-driven places, that the mode of discourse in a particular passage vary into other modes. What I'm trying to get you to do—though the details will be organically driven, as they are not now; and though the details will have yearning as their center of gravity or engine, as they do not now—nevertheless, that moment-to-moment sensual flow is your normal mode of speaking in literary fiction. As hard as it is. If you think this is hard, where you're free to make up anything, what if your choices are circumscribed by all the other detailed choices you've already made? See, this is what you're buying into, folks, coming to this university and wanting to be an artist.

ROB: Mary Jane is going to do hers now. OK, Mary Jane and everyone else, get into your space. I think I'd like to take you into the corridor approaching the room where you must identify your father. So take a moment and get yourself there; and pick me up in the corridor, in the moment and through the senses, very close to coming into his presence. [She does not respond.] All right, let's put you just inside the door. You have just opened the door to the room where he's been held. Place yourself in the room.

Mary Jane: I'm standing in a door frame looking into a room that is completely black.

ROB: You've summarized that to a fair degree. Let's put you in that door frame and I want you literally to be the camera's eye. Look off to your extreme left, because there's a little sound. Something draws your attention. Or a bit of light to the left. You focus on that, and then swing your eye moment-to-moment back to wherever your father is.

Mary Jane: It's like looking into a cave.

ROB: OK, you understand the problem with that? Yeah. Let's see something. And if you've got to put a little more light in this room, do so. Let's just take that last step into the room; give me that motion and then stop yourself and then your eyes fall on one thing.

Mary Jane: I step into the room. I can feel my brother right behind me.

ROB: How? Let's do this: let's put you in that door frame again. I want you to take a moment and be in your body there. Now, tell me about how you know your brother is behind you. How do you feel him? Where do you feel him?

Mary Jane: I have a sense of his presence over my shoulder. [She laughs.]

ROB: What is that sense?

Mary Jane: Maybe it's a smell.

ROB: Maybe it is. Let's go back into your body there, OK? And just wait upon it. You don't have to rush answers.

Just get into your body and stay in that doorway and if that room in front of you is dark, tell me where on your body you feel the darkness.

Mary Jane: In the center of my chest.

ROB: Tell me where in your body you sense your brother. Wait for it.

Mary Jane: Behind my shoulders.

ROB: Yes, but what part of your shoulders and what is the feeling on your shoulders?

Mary Jane: A sensation of warmth.

ROB: Is there really? Are your shoulders bare?

Mary Jane: It's March.

ROB: Don't try to remember, OK? In this moment that you're inventing now, imagine it.

Mary Jane: Yes, because I'm wearing a sundress. In front, it's very cold. There's a patch of warmth.

ROB: That's good. See where your father is now.

Mary Jane: There's a spot of light in the room, almost like it's been . . .

ROB: Where is it first, before you tell me what it's like.

Mary Jane: It's shining intensely on his head and illuminating the casket that he's lying in.

ROB: You're generalizing now. OK, a spot of light comes from where to where? It falls from point A to point B, and in point B what do you see in full detail? Give me that in a few sentences.

Mary Jane: Where it falls from?

ROB: I just want you to see it and tell me what you see, because there is a sense of that light moving from a place to a place, isn't there? The source of light is one place—I want your eyes to go first to the bright light above, and then follow it and see something.

Mary Jane: On his face. His face is an odd ash gray color and the shape of his face is not . . . there's a twist to his jaw and his mouth that doesn't look anything like him.

ROB: You've analyzed the twist of his jaw. Let me see the twist of his jaw right now.

Mary Jane: The twist of his jaw, his mouth, it looks as if someone had cupped their hand around his jaw and pushed up.

ROB: OK. I want you to have a flash of memory in this moment. You see that face flash to something, some memory of that face.

Mary Jane: Well, in the moment that he died, his jaw fell open.

ROB: OK, you've just summarized that. Go from a specific, in-the-moment, concrete, sensual encounter with the face before you in the funeral home to a specific in-the-moment encounter with that other moment. I know this is tough stuff. It's tough for you personally, and the sense impressions we're getting at are very challenging in themselves, but so are they always, when you do them right. So let's back up: clear your consciousness. One more time, evoke the face in the funeral home, and then evoke the face that you saw in the moments before his death. Don't try to remember what you said; I want you to see it afresh and just be there with it. I want to get both faces from you in the same flow.

Mary Jane: His chin and his lips and his nose looked as

if someone had grabbed ahold and shoved them into a mask. The face that I remember from the moment of his death is soft.

ROB: Soft where?

Mary Jane: The chin was elastic. There was still mobility . . .

ROB: You're analyzing and generalizing here. Let's just look at something on his face. Let's look into his eyes before he dies; look into his eyes.

Mary Jane: His eyes are almost completely closed. There's some movement in the lids, a little water.

ROB: Look at his mouth. What's his mouth doing?

Mary Jane: His mouth is partially open.

ROB: Partially, what does that mean?

Mary Jane: Half open.

ROB: Do you see his teeth, his tongue? What do you see?

Mary Jane: You see his tongue. You see his lower teeth.

ROB: What are they like?

Mary Jane: They're yellow.

ROB: Yellow like what?

Mary Jane: Like old piano keys.

ROB: What do you smell?

Mary Jane: Room freshener.

ROB: OK, but what's that smell?

Mary Jane: Flowery.

ROB: Flowery, like what?

Mary Jane: Flowery, like jasmine. In bloom.

ROB: I can't buy that one. It's trying to smell like jasmine in bloom. What's it really smell like?

Mary Jane: Actually, the flowery jasmine room freshener is not doing a very good job of covering up . . .

ROB: You don't have to analyze it. There is that smell but layered under it is . . .

Mary Jane: The smell of old sweat and intense concentrated urine smell.

ROB: All right, that's fine. Thank you, Mary Jane.

It's tough. When you focus on this detail and that—his mouth, a smell. We had some nice things there. It's easy to get spooked doing this; very quickly you become conscious of how difficult and demanding it is, and then often your response to that stress is to start forcing it, willing it. The voice in your head that I talked about a few weeks ago starts going, "Oh, that's not good enough. This isn't working, is it? Better turn it up a notch." And then it falls apart.

But look, it's this way for everybody. Janet and I struggle with the same things every day. We fight off those impulses to will this, to analyze and describe it with technique. We get the same kind of panicky feeling when it's not quite there. You just have to learn to let it go, to stay loose with it.

Even if we're not fighting off serious emotion, this is still tough, isn't it? Just moving through space in the moment is very tough, it really is—but necessary, as I hope you're convinced. All right, Brandy, do you want to do it? Let's put you on the seesaw. Things are going OK. Let's do an up and down. Can we do that in the moment?

Brandy: The air is hot against the back of my neck as it blows my hair up as I go down.

ROB: You're at the top. Let's do a slow motion, and you're about to go down. Let's start you there. Put us on that seat of the seesaw with you and bring us down. So, you are sitting where?

Brandy: My legs are straight out in front of me. The seat is hard wood, the paint is slick, so at the top I'm almost sliding forward.

ROB: Where do you feel that?

Brandy: On the back of my thighs the paint chips dig in a little bit. And on the sides I can feel the handle that I'm also grabbing onto.

ROB: Let's put your hands on the handle. What does that feel like?

Brandy: It's hot metal, worn smooth on top.

ROB: Glance off—where are you looking? What do you see?

Brandy: Trees to my right.

ROB: You just summarized that for me. See the tree. I turn my eyes to the right and . . . what've you got?

Brandy: The leaves are brown and crusty, but it's still pretty full, and I can't see all the branches.

ROB: That's what you can't see. I don't have a shape yet to that tree. You're a little girl. You're on a seesaw. You're up high, and when you go up high you love to let your gaze travel out to the world from a height that you're rarely at. And there's a tree. So let me see the tree through your eyes.

Brandy: The first thing I see is the leaves.

ROB: You just generalized that for me. I doubt if the first

thing you see is the leaves unless the tree is at arm's length. What kind of tree is it?

Brandy: It's an oak tree.

ROB: Yes, oak tree's good; that's a concrete detail. What is the configuration of the great branches on this oak tree? An oak tree doesn't grab you first by its leaves, does it?

Brandy: Knobby branches?

ROB: You saw this wonderful tree and you want to tell me about this tree. I think you're just a little bit spooked now. It's really simple. Just think of the most beautiful, wonderful oak tree you've ever seen and let that be growing off to your right when you're at the height of this seesaw. You've just lifted and your thighs are prickled by the paint chips and your hands are warmed by the metal handle that you're grasping tightly and you lift your face and turn your eyes and what do you see? [Silence.] OK, let the tree go. Look down the seesaw at your brother. Let me see your brother through your eyes as you're at the apogee of your seesawing.

Brandy: He has tight brown curls of hair, his mouth is open.

ROB: How so?

Brandy: Like he's going to scream or yell. It's like he's taking a big breath.

ROB: What's in his eyes? What are his eyes like?

Brandy: They're brown and very wide-open. He looks very excited.

ROB: "Excited" is an abstraction. But OK. He's just flexed his legs, he's pushed off, and you begin to fall. Tell me what you feel.

Brandy: My stomach jumps to my throat. I feel kind of like I'm lifted off the seat for a minute.

ROB: It's like you're lifted off the seat for a minute— that's kind of generalized. Let's feel that sensation with you. In fact you are lifted off, aren't you? And how do you feel that letting go? Where in your body do you feel the lift.

Brandy: My legs kind of unstick.

ROB: Good, OK.

Brandy: And it's cooler, like there's air.

ROB: A sudden rush of coolness on your thighs as you lift off, right? The prickles are gone and the air replaces them, yes? Where else in your body?

Brandy: My hands are kind of pulled away. They're not gripping as tight, they're pulled to the fingers.

ROB: What do you smell? Do you smell sweat?

Brandy: Yeah.

ROB: What else?

Brandy: A metallic smell.

ROB: What do you hear? What's the sound in your ears?

Brandy: Like a wind or a breath, or . . .

ROB: OK, thank you, Brandy. Even if we're not fighting off serious emotion, this is still tough, isn't it? There were some very good things coming there.

All right, Leslie, let's send you out into the field. You're following your brother into the field. Give us that moment.

Leslie: Let me just say my brother's name is Prince. It's a family name.

ROB: The brother formerly known as Prince. [Laughter.] Or actually known as Prince. Say anything you want to after approaching the bales.

Leslie: The grass is deep and wet and grainy with seeds and Prince's head and arms rise up against the white sky washed with red, black as if he were part of the hill beyond.

ROB: How's he moving?

Leslie: The rows of hay bales like a row of animals against the sky. Prince wades through the grass with his arms outstretched as if he were walking through deep water.

ROB: What part of your own body are you most aware of at the moment?

Leslie: The dampness from the tall grass has wet my legs and shorts, but the cold rises up my stomach like a button being pulled on a drawstring from my sacrum up into the center of my chest, and I shiver.

ROB: Where?

Leslie: Pulling my arms into the sleeves of my T-shirt, wrapping them around my chest as I jump over the grass to catch up to him.

ROB: A flash of memory now.

Leslie: But he's running too fast. And in the darkness I imagine that if I were to catch him and grab the back of his T-shirt something frightening would happen.

ROB: You're starting to analyze too much for this exercise, OK? *Frightening* is also being abstract. You've just shivered, trying to keep up, and you see him quite wonderfully, vividly before you, and the rows of bales like animals are out there. Just go straight to another concrete moment in the past like this. It could be the distant past. Just something comes to you, OK?

Leslie: I found the puppy on the hilltop beyond the hay bale . . .

ROB: Don't summarize, OK? Let's see the very moment you see the puppy.

Leslie: In a swirl of grass, as if it had bedded down as it squirmed to move, its legs broken, flies swarming in its ears and eyes . . .

ROB: Let's look at the leg more closely. See, you've analyzed the leg for me. I want to see the leg with you. In the very moment you perceive it's broken, I want to see it.

Leslie: Against the orange fur there was a deeper red, a black hole, where the puppy had been . . .

ROB: Don't analyze it, that's enough. What part of your own body are you conscious of now, seeing that puppy?

Leslie: The breath rushes out of me, and I stumble back so that the puppy is lost in the grass.

ROB: Link that to a parent, an image of a parent.

Leslie: My mother's eyes looked dark in the shape of fish with streaks running out of them down her cheeks.

ROB: Where are you? Look around. Look away from your mother's face and see something.

Leslie: In the rick of rotted pine beside the back door we heard the cat weeping. She, my mother, stepped down the concrete steps and reached for one silver stick of wood as if she were afraid it would collapse when she moved one piece.

ROB: That's a little bit of an analysis. Show me her body and her body language; have them reveal that she's afraid. Tell me how you perceive in the moment through the senses.

Leslie: She bends and leans, swaying on the edge of the step, touching the rough corner of the stick with just her forefinger, testing its balance in the pile.

ROB: What part of your body are you most aware of now?

Leslie: My feet seem a long way away from me, as if I were very tall, but my head feels heavy.

ROB: Hear the cat again. Hear it more clearly in an extended way.

Leslie: The noise seems to come from inside the ribs, just a handful of ribs, a small noise that seems torn, already broken beyond repair.

ROB: Now what part of your body are you feeling?

Leslie: It's as if I swallow something sharp. I swallow and swallow and it won't go down.

ROB: Come back to your brother now. He does something; let's see him do a specific different thing now.

Leslie: Prince runs into the bale, digs his foot just above the coiled center, launches up onto the top as if he were running against the sky, his arms spread out, his thin hair wisping around his head, each finger spread like a feather.

ROB: Let him turn and face you; see his face.

Leslie: It's too dark to see his face, but the sunset is reddish on the side of his cheek.

ROB: Red like what? [Long pause.] Reincorporate. Red like what?

Leslie: Red like blood in a sink.

ROB: OK. Thank you, Leslie.

That was very good, thank you, Leslie. This is what I'm getting at. Couldn't have planned it better. [Laughter.] Look, if it didn't work for you tonight, don't feel bad about it. This is really tough. You're approaching an awareness that you haven't been led to before but that is an essential basic skill. You must be masters of the sensual moment. These questions I've asked—when, in fact, you can range anywhere—are much less demanding than the questions your work will ask of you under similar circumstances. You must move your characters from here to there. They have to be in the moment, and they have to look into a face and see something, and you cannot analyze it, and you cannot abstract it. You're in the sensibility of the character, and you must be in the moment in terms of that character, and also there in terms of the rest of the piece. But what we've done tonight is artificial in many ways, and if it didn't work for you, don't feel bad about it. Just open up the negotiations between you and your unconscious and your computer. You'll make a lot of mistakes, and that's OK. It's part of the process of getting to where you want to go.

Actually, all of you had very good moments. None of you was up here without at least a few very good moments, and I hope you felt what you tapped into briefly when you were inventing, recombining, in the sensual moment.

9

THE WRITTEN EXERCISE

"You have to be available to the invisible
voices that are swirling around you."
—George C. Wolfe

Tonight we're going to do on the page exactly what we did last week orally; that is, to write moment by moment through the senses only. This will be a coached writing exercise in seven stages. I'll give you the first stage and you'll begin to write; then I'll drop in six more times, each time to give you another step. It's important not to go beyond the parameters of what I tell you to do. When I describe a new stage, if you've not finished the previous one, note the new instructions in the margin, then go back to where you were, pick that up, and move as quickly as you can to the new stage.

Don't run ahead, though. Stay within the boundaries of each instruction. Once again: no abstraction, no generalization, no summary, no analysis, no interpretation. Force yourself to write moment to moment through the senses only. Don't hassle your style at this point, don't agonize over just the right word; just keep the flow of it through the senses—

flowing, flowing, flowing. Don't think, don't think. Senses, senses, senses. If you really do that rigorously, you'll find your-self flowing right down—at least into the foyer of—this great house that is your unconscious.

I want you to write in the first person. When I say "you," I am referring to your character.

Now, about the character. If you have a character you're working with closely, you may write from the viewpoint of that character, but I'm reluctant to encourage this, because if that character happens to be one you're willing into being, then the exercise will not be very useful to you. In the ab-sence of any character you feel a desperate need to get in touch with, I urge you to write through a character with demographics very similar to your own. This is not you, this is not autobiography, but unless you've got a really burning character that you need to explore, then the character you choose needs to be very close to you in age, gender, ethnicity, and so forth.

If you get to the end of a stage before I come in, don't write ahead, and don't go back and start rewriting; just put your pen down and meditate. I'll notice if there are a lot of pens down, and I'll jump in. It's likely, though, that if you finish these stages before I get to the next, you're not giving it enough intense moment-to-moment attention. In that case, try to focus more intently on the next stage.

When you finish the piece and feel done, just close your notebook and pick up your pen and go away. At some point if there are only a few of you left we may decide that you need to take your piece home and finish it later. I wouldn't think that you'd be able to bear spending more than an hour and a half on this, if you do it as intensely as you should.

Let's start. Here's your first stage.

[Editor's note: what follows are the seven stages of the exercise, succeeded by three examples of the results from the class on the evening when the exercise was recorded.]

The seven stages:

1. You awake abruptly, though it isn't morning, and you're not in a bed. But you are in the place where you live. The room where you awake is rich in objects and their associations. You are breathless and anxious from a dream you can't, and won't, remember. You look around the room, everything in it shaped by an unspecified anxiety. Let's see the room, in the moment, through the senses.

2. One object in particular catches your attention and suggests a strong connection to your anxiety. Move toward that object; touch it; experience it sensually.

3. The object evokes a memory as vivid as a dream but not the one you woke from. It is a real memory, one based on wanting, desiring something. But this is a surface thing you want—an object, a gesture, a touch, whatever. Focus on the moment-to-moment, specific memory of desiring this thing, which, nevertheless, carries an intimation of deeper yearning. But don't go to that deeper desire yet. Experience the surface thing through your · character's sensibility.

4. Now let the memory of this want include a moment when a second memory is evoked. This second memory

involves another object, different from the one you are touching in the present time but similar to it in its basic sensual pattern. This second memory surprises you. You deeply connect it to the first. And the *wanting* suddenly goes deeper, into a state of being, a state of self. Don't label it. Play it out in the moment through the senses.

5. In that second memory you are moved to an action, driven by your yearning. Let the action happen moment to moment.

6. Some part of the action will bring you back to the present, to an awareness of the first object. Reexperience the object. Your sensual perception of it is altered, reshaped by the emotion and yearning you have experienced in these two linked memories.

7. Now, back in the present, in the light of all this, you take an action.

The examples:

Rita Mae Reese

Magnets

A small spot of the green Formica table and the left corner of my mouth is slick with my warm drool. What woke me up? How did I fall asleep here? Outside the kitchen window is just darkness crouching and I can hear the hum of the little fluorescent light twitching over the sink, full of dirty dishes, but nothing else. There is no other sound in the house. The round white clock's hands say 5:16 but its battery ran out weeks ago. I look at the microwave but it isn't programmed. I'm sweating, my mouth is horrible, like I've been siphoning gasoline with it. I push the chair away from the table, noticing the letter I'd pushed to the other side before falling asleep. The white paper with its rows of neat black ink strains up from its creases like a tired child unwilling to go to sleep.

   I ignore it and walk across the sticky linoleum. Had I spilled something? I open the fridge door and the light is too bright even in this brightly lit room. My heart kicks and I can almost see a scene—something slithers from the back of my neck, through my throat, and stops at my larynx. My mind struggles to see—some dream fragment, repulsive and indistinct. I stare at the carton of milk, the cartons of leftovers, and the little round jar of horseradish. What had I dreamed? I felt like I'd missed something important, the bus back home or a lover's last call. Is that what I'd dreamed?

   I grab the carton of milk and it slips from my hands, the white ghostness of it splashing on my legs and over the dirty yellow linoleum. I bite my lip. I will not cry. I shut the door a little too forcefully and Jill's picture that she'd drawn of me and Sam slides with its magnet down and flutters into the milk. I crouch down and put the drawing on the table, after blotting it against my dress.

   I pick the carton of milk up—there is still some inside— and put it back in the fridge. I wipe up the milk with paper towels and as I stand up to go to the trash can, my bare foot comes down on something cold and hard. It is the magnet. I pick it up and instead of just putting it back on the fridge, I sit down with it still in my hand. I hear the neighbor's dog bark, twice. I lift my head and listen but the house is still quiet. The magnet is an old-fashioned valentine, fifties-style cornball romance, a smiling orange saying "Orange you glad you're mine, valentine?" on metal, heavily laminated.

Sam had been on a magnet-making kick, and took any-thing she got her hands on—old stamps, postcards, cards, pic-tures—and turned them into an endless stream of magnets. Sam was with Diana then and I remember seeing them in their kitchen together, Diana was doing the dishes and Sam leaned into her in a way that made my own back feel cold and exposed. I thought of what it would be like to have Sam's lips on my neck, warm, laughing into my skin over some private joke. I pretended to look at the books on their shelves in the dining room, a good fifty square feet of shelving displaying *Foxfire* books, Marion Zimmer Bradley's entire body of work, and a lot of Quality Paperback selections. I was going to ask Diana if she wanted help washing up from the dinner they'd made for me, the new single girl at work. Diana at work is perfect and I admit I'd sort of hoped her home life was different but it was worse. Her girlfriend Sam was beautiful and handsome, with olive skin, an aquiline nose, and eyes that really looked at a person. She repeated my name when we were introduced and asked me what I thought of St. Petersburg. She looked in my eyes as I stumbled over the an-swer, revising it for her approval as I went along. I looked down, just to avoid her eyes, and saw the best mouth I'd ever stared at—a little smirk, with the lightest laugh line on the left. I thought of kissing her then but told myself that I'd been with-out a girlfriend for too long.

Holding the magnet, so square and so dense, a nice hard weight in the center of my palm now. Sam's mother had a laugh line just like hers in that little picture, the only picture, Sam had of her. I remember going to Sam's apartment after she'd moved out of Diana's, the sparseness of the furnishings— a rocker, a table and chairs, a dresser, a bed, a stereo, and one set of bookshelves. She kept her books boxed up by the wall next to the front door. On her dresser she had a photo of Diana (it hurt me every time I saw it but I'd never asked her to take it down) and the tiny photo in the metal frame of her mother. I'd picked it up while she was in the kitchen, making us dinner. I'd gone to the bathroom and since her bedroom door was open, I stepped inside, amazed at the austerity of the room— the unmade bed, the clean floor, the bare walls, the dresser with its two pictures. I'd lifted the picture of her mother, cupped it in my hands and lifted it to my face as if I were smelling it. I have no idea why. "That's my mother," her voice came over my shoulder and I jerked, put it back on the dresser, nearly knocking over the picture of Diana. Sam reached her arm around me and picked it up.

"Sorry," I mumbled, my face hot.

She didn't say anything. "She's beautiful," I offered and Sam nodded. She put the picture back down and for a moment I was afraid she'd pick up the picture of Diana and I couldn't stand that, I'd have to leave, and I desperately wanted to stay. "She looks like you," I smiled, trying to show I meant to harm.

"You think?" Sam wrinkled her nose, cocked her head. Is she playing with me?

"Your mouth," I began and floundered.

She smiled, ducking her head.

"You have the same mouth," I continued.

"Thank you," she paused, looking at me like I might be about to pass out and I might have. "Do you want some wine? That's why I came looking for you, to ask if you wanted some wine."

"I'm sorry. I'm sorry about Diana. I've really fucked things up for you and I should leave."

"What do you want, Dee?"

I smiled helplessly, looking at the picture of her mother as if for guidance. She took a step closer. We were a foot away from each other. I smelled her lavender soap, her deodorant, a piney-clean scent, I could even smell the Carmex on her lips.

"I want to be with you," I said and didn't just mean it euphemistically. I do, I want to fuck her, I want to sleep with her, I want to wake up with her, but I want to just be with her too. Just sit very still with her sitting very still beside me and know that we are the only two people who belong in that room, who are wanted in that room.

"Why?" she asked, and I laughed. *Why* is never the right question to ask about sex. *How*, maybe. *When*, sure. *Where*, that can be an issue. Even *what* has its place if you know where to shop and you aren't timid. But *why*?

"Is that a 'no'?"

She grabbed my hand and led me to the kitchen, which smelled of basil and garlic and was warmer than the rest of the house. She poured wine into the two glasses on the counter without letting go of my hand. "You have through dinner to tell me why," she said and raised her glass to mine before we drank.

I'm still thirsty, sitting at the table with the smiling orange-head magnet no longer cold in my hand. I squeeze it hard. It leaves dents in the flesh of my fingers. The orange face, faded to the color of Tang with too much water, grins up at me as if we share some embarrassing secret. "Orange you glad you're mine?" I hear the front door open. Sam's home. The *why* from my memory echoes in my head.

I pick up the picture of me and Sam drawn by her daughter. Jill has drawn the laugh line on Sam's face. It is a good likeness. I put it back on the fridge. I pick up the letter and crumple it up, stuff it beneath the milk-wet paper towels. I climb the stairs to our bedroom and find Sam already undressed, already in bed.

Christie Grimes

Stone

I fell asleep on the futon again. When I woke, my eyes darted to the muted TV and I wondered what could have woken me. I felt an ache in my chest as if all my muscle were taut against my breastbone. The dingy carpet was in the shadows but I spied pieces of tortilla chips that had been brushed from the coffee table in a feeble attempt to clean. My back and muscles ached. The muscles in my calves were tight from being rigid, poised, ready for some type of assault or flight. I smelled a faint odor of furniture polish which fit oddly into the forgotten dusty apartment. I rolled my head to the side feeling the creases on my face. I worked my jaw, slowly unclenching it and loosing the muscles. The clock on the bookcase read 4:00 and Oprah was smiling at a guest. The small marble cat on my coffee table appeared to grin at me in the shadows, its green eyes flittering in their purple housing. The cat was the last gift I had received from a man. Not a potential lover, mind you, he was married, had three children, and told stories about how he brought his wife a flower each day until she fell in love with him. He had given me the cat the day I left. Something he saw in the store and thought of me. Our relationship had always clicked. He would have bailed me out of jail or picked me up at the hospital, but I never would have asked. Our relationship was strictly work. His shaggy too long hair hung in his eyes when we hugged and wrestled, and I knew that he cared about me like an adoring brother, or maybe a what-might-have-been look with a smile. I treasured that purple cat, but today it spooked me. The toothy smile did not seem playful, it was sinister. The whiskers blowing from the air vent made the plastic come alive and twitch at me. I pulled the small blanket up to my chin and tucked my feet under me, locking the blanket into a sleeping bag comfort. I glanced up at a picture adorning my bookcase which I took alone at the top of a mountain. No one would climb the formation with me to see the spectacular view of green, yellow, and auburn tones. The picture did not show my smiling face, nor anyone else's. I had pocketed a chunk of granite on the way down. It was larger than my hand and heavy in my pack, but the grainy wholeness of the rock felt more real than the picture, and it gave me comfort even when I felt the solitude of not being able to share the moment with another. The rock lay at the base of my bookcase crammed between particleboard and the wall. I walked over to it, shuffling my coarse feet across the carpet, creating a scratching sound. I picked up the rock and rolled it from palm to palm, small particles of dirt and crystal attaching to my hands. I rubbed my forefinger over the black streak creating a jagged Z through the center of the beige and gray rock. My fingers traced the letter, feeling the smooth black penetrating. It felt coarser, more raw than the granite exterior. I rubbed my fingers into it, softly scraping my index finger, enjoying the painful sensation in my skin. Still holding the rock in my left hand, I gently swung my arm up, feeling the lift of the weight of the rock. My finger wandered to the blunt edge of the back of the rock. On the floor it balanced flat, raised in a trapezoid shape with the black only visible in a small streak on the top and only completely visible in design from underneath. I had almost ruined the Z by breaking the rock. I hurled it the last time he left me. He walked through the door leaving me only with myself. No answers, no accommodations, and no love, understanding, or kindness on his face. I wanted answers. I thought I could fix everything if he would only let me kiss him, grab him by his large arms and trace his lips with my tongue. Slowly, erotically seducing him, sucking on his lower lip and forcing my tongue into his mouth probing for answers. But he pulled away, taking a backward step toward the door when I tried to push my body into his and against the wall. Instead he turned to the side like a matador and he left me. Motionless without a grip, I saw his hand reach behind him and I stood tense, afraid to spook him. He glanced at me, at my body rather than my eyes and his head started to shake but he stilled it, cocking it instead. He opened the door, sidestepping through it and quietly pulling it shut, clicking into the door frame. I stood for a moment before crumbling to the ground. It was no use chasing him. I knew when he would not look at my eyes. I felt it in my chest, a strange tightening, a hope coiling around nothing, pulling tighter and tighter trying to capture something so thin that it cannot be grasped. That is when I walked to the window and stood at the edge, trying to see out the corner of the blinds without moving them and without being seen. I could only see the dark headlights of his car as it reversed out of view. I felt angry, humiliated, and defeated. I backed away from the window into the bookcase and tripped into the rock, stubbing my large toe. I hopped backward and seized the rock, hurling it with my arm and my body into a shot-putter stance and flinging it into the floor where it bounced on the hard ceramic tile, breaking a quarter inch off the side into a crumbling piece and shattering the tile beneath it into cracked jagged pieces. I walked over to the rock and carefully rolled it over, afraid to see what I had done. I saw the dirt and residue on my hand and the small black shards falling off in dust. I looked for the Z. Once I brushed it clean, it was still there, only slightly torn, a small piece of the end of the rock still had the black streak but now that flat surface was no longer level, it was split into several layers of rocky slope down a path of granite. I breathed out, he never even knew what that rock meant.

We shopped for rings one time, halfheartedly joking but serious in that way that you hope it will be right, that you hope that you are not imagining things, that you are wanted and loved and protected. So, we window-shopped which took us into a jewelry store where I saw the ring that would mean it for me. Like choosing the cup of life or death, it was a test. We walked through the display cases promising eternal love for any price, the greater the amount, the greater the result did not add up in my estimate. I dragged my fingers across the glass cases leaving trails of smears behind. He followed me, rubbing my shoulder and leaning into my back, pressing me into the case until I laughed. When I first walked around, I spotted it. A small band interlaced with weaving. Like serpents braided together in a loop, the lace a continuous Escher connection in a Celtic pattern. He ambled to the other side of the store browsing among crosses and ID bracelets and finally asked to see an elaborate ring made of smooth white gold. Its pale color disguising its value. He turned it over in his fingers and winked at me. The ring had a large diamond inset in the middle with two small emeralds on either side. It sickened me. My stomach felt gassy and my breath lacked oxygen, as if breathing through a filter. He held it out to me and I touched the fold, cold to my finger and hollow and light in my palm.

"Try it on, seven and a quarter, right? It should fit."

I shook my head, hoping my fingers had grown fatter, that it would not slip over my knuckle. This hope left me when he took my hand and gently looked into my eyes and smiled, his cheeks tightening, his eyes crinkling at the edges. I felt the band slide onto my finger effortlessly. He lifted my hand to my eyes and I felt a band go around my heart.

"What do you think?"

"Is this the one that you like best?"

"I came in last week and had it fitted for you."

I thought about the effort that he had put into it, but it didn't fit. It did not fit my heart, my head, or any other part of my body. My finger felt alien to me as I looked at it. I slowly reached up and disentangled my hand, sliding the ring off and placing it in his hand. I smiled.

"Let's look some more, shall we? It's beautiful but I'd really like something simple."

He snorted and then his mouth hung open and his eyebrows raised as he realized I was serious. I absently popped my ring finger, massaging the area where the ring had set.

"Look over here, for instance. What do you think of this one?" I led him back to the small silver case, pointing at the ring displayed in a velvet prop.

"That's just a plain old ring. Why would you want it?"

I shrugged and asked to see it. I took it and rolled it between my fingers, feeling the bumps and holes between the intertwined metal ropes. The outer edge was smooth but I pressed my finger into the pattern. My skin seeped through. I released the ring between my index finger and my palm and I looked at the tiny snake pattern it had left. I tried to place it on my finger but it was too small and would only loosely slip onto my pinky finger.

"I like it because it means something."

"Means what? What meaning is there in a cheap piece of silver? That says a lot to me."

I looked up and stared into his brown eyes. His brow was furrowed and he looked at me with a mixture of amusement and patronizing knowledge that he knew me better than I knew myself. I placed the ring on the counter and let it twirl in a small circle, rattling before I led him out of the store. We went home that night and tried to make love but there was a wall. His skin felt synthetic and his kisses forced. I was content to lie there within myself knowing me and realizing that he did not.

I felt the same chill now. My skin loose and the air chilling me internally as I sat the rock on the ground and rocked it back into place with my big toe. I rubbed my hand across my throat and let it rest on my chest. He had come the closest to penetrating my armor, getting past my skin, my tough hide, and all of the challenges that I placed for him to prove himself. He passed. But after all that he had not reached me. He had only reached someone that he thought was me. And, maybe it had been.

I sat with my knees hugged to my chest and rocked slightly, pushing the rock with me. I tilted it out onto its broken side and let it fall heavily back to its resting place. I could run my entire foot across its top and lift the base by lifting my heel, pointing my toes down when I arched my foot. The black streak was barely visible, showing and then disappearing as I rocked it and stopped as I leaned forward with the rock raised. The floor was hard beneath me and I leaned into the wall beneath the windowsill. With a quick thrust of force from my foot, I pushed the rock against the wall, stuck and exposed, the beautiful black marble visible, smooth and worn. It was covered by the granite, rough and crumbling. Years of sediment piled onto it, covering the delicate beauty hidden beneath the coarse exterior.

My toe rubbed a piece of the black edge and I wondered if I wasn't better without him. The colors of the granite swirl in some areas and the drab colors hide the vivid pure black underneath. The black rock feels powerful, and the rock surrounding it poor and dry. The light granite color was a mask of ugly plain mountain, deceptive and tamed. I stood and left the rock propped upward against the wall, revealing the jagged black design underneath. I walked to the door and opened it. I stepped out into the hallway, the dirty runner cold beneath my feet. Barefoot, I walked outside my building and stepped onto the cement. Stepping gingerly around loose stones and pebbles, I looked across the lot and felt the cool air brushing my skin. Taking a deep breath, I felt the air chill and burn my lungs. I felt the breath in my fingertips and my toes. I stood on my tiptoes, pressing my feet into the cold pavement. I scanned the area and walked over to a large curb. I sat beneath a tree and crossed my ankles, staring at the ground. Amid pine needles and gravelly rocks, there were small pebbles and stones that had blown to their resting place. I leaned over and brushed my fingers through them. I picked up a small red stone. It was smooth and had shades of burnt red and orange swirling across its smooth surface. I rolled the cold stone in my hand and closed my hand over the stone, embracing the color.

Gay Milner

Marzipan

Gunshot. What? I must have fallen asleep; the red patch burns on my thigh against the Naugahyde. It's hot, and the air damp with stickiness that belongs to this landlocked land. The gunshot?—yes—*The Virginian*, that blond boy Travis, snub nose and cupid mouth on the other side of the smoking barrel. But the grainy black-and-white, the grainy sound (a soup of music) is just the faded image of some more violent dream. I can't hold it. I pull myself hand over hand back into it because I must save myself, or her, or it. What did I need to do? A lump of failure in my chest.

Over the cowboys a cheap cardboard frame sits on the fake wood of the TV set, little gold pressed curlicues around a snapshot of Dogzilla, his rich red hair curly on his ears that hang like a pageboy to his thin black smile. Irish setter as coed circa 1958. And is that my only personal memento, the only photograph worth bringing after thirty-five years? What was that dream? I'm a cowgirl, my dog has been abducted by a rustler; crap. What creature is it that I must save?

I balance myself, pain slicing up from my spine across my right hip socket, unsteady on my feet, and hobble to the front door, swing the squeaky screen. On the porch—knobbled knuckles of my stockinged feet on the red cement—I reach for the post and am overcome with dread. This porch support is a double cylinder of painted metal, held ten inches or so apart by (also painted, rusting white) metal shapes: a series of interlocking tendrils, leaves, two birds in flight. Where it disappears into the clapboard ceiling it has been patched with grainy putty. Its two feet are buried in the red cement. The grain of the paint grates on my fingertips.

I look "into the eyes" of this flat white metal bird, and there tumbles out of the hot void where the dream has fled a moment from Liège. I was—what?—no more than eight or nine because the market was still there, and yet there was some fear attached to food, the possibility of want. Nine, then. 1939. My mother's hip warm against my shoulder in a coat of loden green. A bird was pecking at the edge of a puddle, at a piece of cake or *petit four*. Yes. My mother was buying bread and I was waiting to see if there would be a marzipan, a biscuit, a *mille-feuille* for me. I was—why?—terrified that I would be ignored, denied, expected to go home without a treat. I wanted to bend and snatch the cake away from the bird, who seemed impossibly bold at my feet. Like the German boys who would not hesitate to say anything— scum! kike! gypsy! This bird had my sweet, unless (her voice murmured above me, the inconsequential murmur of the housewife and the merchant, his deeper, dulcet, reasoning plaints mixed in with hers)—unless she would remember me. Why did I both suppose that they could feed me and fear that they would not? The bird cocked a beady eye at me. Taunting. An ordinary small brown bird, fat with feathers, who might yet pluck out my eyes.

My mother said, "Simone. M. Partenier is speaking to you."

Partenier. The name comes back unbidden, the *pâtissier* of the open market. His banner ran along his stall at the level of my knees in red scrolling script that I could read: *Partenier Patisserie*. In front of that the malevolent bird sat pecking at the *petit four*, shaking it like a dog with a sock (like Dogzilla my only darling, my only offspring, whom I have abandoned).

"Say thank you to M. Partenier." Who handed down a plain crust of day-old roll. Betrayed, I couldn't speak.

I grasp the metal pole and feel its contour on my palm, turn my palm on its painted surface, feel the white sides of the hospital bed before they wheeled me in. It was a tube of just such stuff. They raised the sides and suddenly my pallet had become a cage. I looked up through the bars and reached up on both sides to hoist myself but my muscles were straw. The beak-nosed nurse told me not to be "irritable now," and some-one—someone else—there were how many in charge of me?—stuck a needle in my arm. My weakness became lightness, I could have floated from my cage, but all the while I knew that this was because they had stolen away my will. They were tak-ing her, I had been tricked. They told me that a broken child was worse than no child at all, but they were tricking me. I rose against the needle, against the bars, against the hand of the nurse who now—thieving bird, big keeper of sweets, hot hip of my mother, abandoned dog—I rose and struck her full in the face.

I think what I said was not intelligible. To myself I said, "I've changed my mind. I'll have the broken one."

"No!" I said to M. Partenier. "I don't want your old crust!" And my mother marched me home and washed my mouth. Soap bittered on my tongue where I had wanted marzipan.

And later, when there was no food, how I would have welcomed a crust of bread. As, now, I would have a deaf child, welcome a heart with a hole in it, see for blind eyes, instead of this none, this nothing, this no one. I have a metal bird and a snapshot of an Irish setter I abandoned. I have a metal pole in my hand, a cement porch, a TV set. The music swells in-side, full of unlikely sugar.

My knuckles ache. I have been gripping the two poles with my two hands. The pain across my back has sharpened with the tensing of my torso. Under my fingers the brushstrokes in the paint—how many coats has somebody applied?—some young couple proud of their clapboard dream and then the landlord hoping to salt away a little nest egg, wanting to be a man of property. The bird does not regard me with its flat eye. There is no malevolence in things. Not even in a hypodermic needle. M. Partenier gave me a crust because the sugar had run out. The bird had probably got a bit of dirty discard and my longing painted it into something precious. I wish I had Dogzilla. But I could not have raised a baby on my own, faulty or whole.

I use the poles to stretch, hanging in an arc against the pain, which pulls my spine, releases, and relaxes. The moon has risen across Oak Alley and tangles in the cottonwood leaves. The dust has dropped with night and left spiced balminess. I turn and go back in, latching the screen behind me.

PART THREE

THE STORIES, ANALYZED

"I do my brand of sumo, and I do my best."
—standard response of sumo wrestlers

10

"FLAMENCO"
BY ERICH SYSAK

Flamenco

It is impossible to escape the heat of the French Quarter. It is searing and ubiquitous, cruel from early June until late September. The few full-time residents of Toulouse and Decatur and St. Peter near City Park stay indoors living lives surrounded by plaster walls and chugging window air conditioners. The insides of things stare back at you. It is hot. This part of the Quarter sits in the soggy apex of an old geographical spoon. It is where artists live. The rent is cheap.

I had come to my father's studio that afternoon to tell him good news, and to ask of him a favor he would not want to fulfill. My girlfriend, Megumi Kido, of one year, had just agreed to marry me. An American would say, *Mey-gumi*. Two syllables and a half-silent *g*. But this is not her name. Her name is Me-gu-mi. Three syllables, each one rising softly in your mouth until the last *e* flutters out like a small bird. It is her secret name. Her real name; her bedroom name.

Since I met her along the bayou at the New Orleans Museum of Art (she sat alone on a plaid blanket to watch mullet jump) she has been the center of my every thought.

For her, I exercise an uncontainable desire to improve, to read prospectuses late at night, to depreciate the adjusted basis of gifts and fair market values ranging as far back as 1946. She understands my craving for things to remain unchanged in our briar, Covington home—the furniture and books, the Kabuki mask and ceramic vase above the fireplace, the silk throw rugs beyond the sofa. She also understands my need to pace, and then to sit quietly and think, sometimes for hours, about the puzzle of numbers a financial accountant must learn the shape of. I am the youngest to make junior partner at Connick, Castelano, Warwick & O'Connor since the Great War. It is a firm with history.

The double shotgun where my parents live needs more than paint. The neighborhood turns pretty around it. It's an old plan to keep thieves away. Vines of bougainvillea breed in the wrought-iron porch rails, and pose against the darkened windows. The old planks, not wide, but delicate and old-fashioned gingerbread, look powdered with white dust and dry. I parallel park behind the Volkswagen van, once my mother's shuttle for doctor's appointments, late-to-school rides, dance recitals, and classes, now with its guts hanging loose below it, reminds the three of us of the chaos of motherhood. Promises have been made to repair it. I step over the stacks of yellow coffee cans, mostly from the Café Du Monde, filled with muddy, mineral spirits and colors, and knock on the studio door before I enter.

It is alleged that Van Gogh's insanity was more than biological. The invisible vapors of mineral spirits inhaled, even swallowed from wet brushes, over time caused his intellect to fail. Inside the studio, these same vapors radiate from the wood floors, the high ceilings where the heat rests, the wet canvas, and the dry stacked arm deep against the walls. All of us have inhaled it over the years.

He sits on a three-legged stool in a cave of paintings. I'm used to the colors, but a stranger is assaulted by it. Your sense of proportion and the familiar, muted tones of the earth, the colors of school buses and buildings, trees and bridges, water, televisions and furniture explode, disappear. His paintings are large, intimidating, colorful, violent, busy, involved. You cannot glance. It takes a while to see them.

He does not turn, but half sits, half stands, juggling the legs of the stool slightly off the ground. He wears no shirt or shoes. There are streaks of red paint on his right arm. His skin is pale. His hair is fine and light gray, tossed up from thinking with his fingers. A box fan twirls near the window where an air conditioner hums. My mother said we look exactly alike. Me at twenty-nine. My father once at twenty-nine. The same. I have seen sketches. It is almost true.

I fall into a vinyl chair near the desk just inside the door, and forget my age.

"I have very good news," I say and cross my hands.

"That would be welcome." His voice is distant. Thinking. Contrary to all logic, it is the best time to speak to him.

"I asked her."

"It's about time."

"She said yes, Dad."

"Congratulations," he says, and offers to shake.

I pull him toward me and gently slap my hand against his soft, sticky back. "I have a favor to ask," I say.

He nods knowingly, but cannot know, and picks through the day's mail at his desk.

"A favor," he repeats to the letters and papers. I look at the painting he's working on and see, through the vastness of time spread out, through the valleys and mountains and creatures within it, a woman, in the distance, on some kind of colorful ledge, a rainbow ledge, and she is dancing. Her hands are posed, fingers snap. She will stomp her right foot in a moment and send catastrophic fissures from her heel.

"Will you paint her?" I ask. The box fan whirs. The air conditioner putters and clicks. From the other side of the shotgun, where my mother lives, I hear her steps on the wooden floor.

"She'll have to sit," he replies.

"Of course," I breathe. "She's so patient, Dad."

Then, from somewhere close, but beyond the universe of my father's studio, a voice materializes. The voice is close. In it there is what can only be called yearning, a friction between the sound, the note, and the ear. It creeps through the windows of the studio: *oh-yeh, oh ya-ya-ya-yaya-u-ya,* and breaks the closure of our deal.

"What is it?" I ask.

"What do you think? He sings. His name is Paco."

"But where?"

"Where? Can't you tell? It's this Jimayna De Alba shit all over again."

The singing stops for a moment, and then continues, just as loudly as before. Jimayna De Alba is my mother's stage name. It is a name that represents her absence from our home. It is time I spent with my father alone. It is how I grew.

My father turns from the painting and points at me with an ox-hair fan brush. "He is singing to her."

"To Mom," I say, knowing already.

He nods and drops the brush into the turpentine. "Yes, for a week now." He looks at the floor, then at me. His blue eyes surprise me. "She quit the studio. I wanted more time with her. It takes her away, not just physically." He cocks his head and considers something quietly.

He has asked my mother to quit. He has asked before. There is nothing I can say to him, though I wish to. It is not the idea, but the words coming out of him. My father does not speak of these things. He does not speak of my mother as the private woman, ever. He does not speak of things inside him, of love, of pain of remembering. Something has changed between us.

"What will you do?" I ask.

"I will paint," he says and points to the canvas.

Then she begins. I feel the vibrations in the floor before I hear it. My mother dances in the next house, where I learned to crawl and speak and run and think. I listen to the clacking, as fast as a card in a bicycle wheel, at times, then hard and final. A thunder in the floor.

* * *

From my mother, I learned this: flamenco borrows from Arabic and Eastern Indian musical rhythms, Spanish and African spirituals, and the Gypsy. It is a guitarist, a singer, and a dancer. They weave a song between them. The guitar is the bridge and the background. The dancer is sung to the floor. Sympathetic, she is held in grief by the voice. The singer kneels to sounds, trills the pieces of the song that call for it. I saw them through the windows of the car, from the back rooms of the dance studio where my mother worked. I heard them do this.

I imagine Paco with his hands, Christlike, palms up, an offering from his chest to my mother where something brews to come out as voice. His eyes are closed. He sits in a wooden chair in an empty room near the windows. His boots tap the floor. The wood shutters are dark, unpainted. And sunlight there, full of dust, touches his white teeth. He sits on the edge of the chair and calls out to who will hear. His singing is devout.

When my parents were younger than I am now, and I was not yet born, people followed my mother to a little club below studio apartments at the corners of Poydras and Decatur, at the fringe of the old Quarter. Ciro's, a small club with doors wide-open at night, spilled music and light into the half-darkened streets. You would walk past and see the crowds—penultimate, staggering groups, cold drinks, laughter. Later, you would also hear the masculine strumming of a flamenco guitar, and then the hard clapping of my mother's shoes on a parquet floor. When the dancer is called, she rises and taps the floor like a drum. She gesticulates. The movements are an expression of temperament. This I know.

My mother learned flamenco at Tulane where she also studied the art of making paper, restoring archival documents, preservation. This is where she met my father, a visiting artist, a devoted painter. She danced weekends and Tuesday nights at Ciro's. But now, Ciro's is boarded over, the studio apartment where she lived above, where my father leaned and watched the crowd adore her, and where it was revealed that she was the most desired woman in all the Quarter at that moment, is empty.

Three days later, we arrive. A boy darts into the street ahead of me, and chases a soccer ball beneath my mother's van. I see his legs V'd beneath the frame, and slow my car to a crawl. I hear my wheels crunching gravel. Megumi smiles and purses her lips in the way she does. Her dark hair is pinned off her neck, and swirls at the crown. We are having children. Her long fingers trace the line of bangs curling above her eyebrows.

"He'll be fine," I say. "I'll be there."

She nods. Her chin gently rises. "I know," she says.

On the porch, at the stoop of my father's door, I see red carnations and white roses draped in paper. When Megumi sees them she captures my hand, thinking that I've put them there for her. I have not. I know they are for my mother, but someone, Paco I assume, has calculated wrong and courted the wrong door.

"They're so fresh," Megumi says, and spreads the flowers beneath her nose.

"There he is," I say and watch my father's silhouette move toward us. I smile. I can't take away her happiness.

The studio floor is swept. The clutter has been stacked into meaningful piles. My father wears a white oxford button-down, khaki shorts, and tennis shoes.

"Welcome," he says warmly, and holds the door for us.

Megumi's yellow dress overwhelms the colors of the paintings. She walks through the rooms toward the kitchen. Suddenly, I look at my father and know he is thinking the same thing.

"My God, I've forgotten how beautiful she is," he says.

"I've never been happier, Dad," I say, watching her appear briefly in the kitchen doorway. "I'm sorry about the flowers."

"What?" He sits at his stool and arranges his colors in little blobs near a large, primed canvas smeared with muted tan and brown.

"They were outside the door," I say.

"Again? He won't give up."

I watch Megumi at the other end of the house, in the kitchen, pulling the flowers from the white sheet, then slicing the stems. She drops aspirin in the water of a large bowl, and then pours in a little 7 UP. Her long fingers pluck at the flower buds and move them like the heads of children for a photograph. Suddenly, she looks up and smiles. I think: these flowers are for my mother.

My father moves the canvas closer to the stool, pulls at his shirt and strokes his chin. I see the wooden window screens open behind him, and through them the close walls of the house next door. Only a narrow alley separates us from Paco. Is Paco her lover? Or does he want her to dance, to return to the studio where a small group of aging musicians gather and recollect?

"Where should she sit?" I ask.

He looks up, surprised, and glances around the studio. "I forgot," he says. "I've never done this."

"Not even for her?" He knows exactly whom I mean.

We pull the vinyl chair from between the two tables. Megumi appears with the bowl and the flowers. "Should I put these on the desk, Mr. Bonnard?" she asks and puts them there before he can answer.

The vinyl chair is arranged near his stool and canvas. Lights are directed toward the coffee-soft cloth. Megumi slips out of her elaborate heels, sits, tucks her legs beneath her, and straightens her dress. She smiles and blinks. The light hits her small shoulders. In the light, little quilts in the fabric around her breasts reveal their intricate stitching. I am standing next to my father, next to the blank canvas and staring with him. We both stare. The old and the new. She is there. Her presence, to me, is suddenly profound, surreal. There is a blue glow in her black hair. I think of turning to my father; this is something he will also know. She is beautiful. But instead, Paco appears between us.

His voice seems louder now. The anguish in his trilling tongue is severe, cracked: *yah-yo-yah-yahahahah-o*. We both turn to the window.

"Sketching a rose," my father says.

"Sketching what? Maybe he's practicing," I say.

"Impossible. She will dance soon."

"Have you talked to her about it?" I ask in a quiet voice. "What does she say?"

As a marine, my father survived nine months in Tu Cung, Vietnam. He was never wounded, nor did he receive any commendations. The pattern is hard to follow. He talked about rivers like the sound of rain. And when it rained he felt as if a river was being dropped on him. His stories are told in chunks. The images aren't clear. I can't picture him in fatigues and boots, holding a rifle and humping a rucksack. Maybe he didn't. Maybe he served in some other capacity.

After the war, and college, and graduate school and teaching, he sold work in the Tate Mitchum Gallery. He was collected and appraised. I have found his name in serious books of art criticism. At times, he visited universities by invitation to speak and to teach. But years have since passed. The Tate Mitchum is closed. The collectors are obscure.

But he still paints. His work has stretched beyond the days of Tate Mitchum. He says he has invented a wholly original process more compatible with human brain chemistry than seratonin. I am not sure what he means, and do not ask. It is not what matters. It does matter that Paco disrupts an already shaky marriage. But one that has lasted through its shakiness, and perhaps because of it, a long time.

* * *

"I married a restoration expert. A practical woman who wanted a kid for Chrissake." He tries to sit at the stool calmly. He sketches the shape of a face and intersects the face with lines.

I move closer to the window, and hear across the alley, the *tink* of glass against glass. Paco's singing slows and moves farther away. I try to imagine what would happen if we simply knocked on the door, confronted him. But it won't happen.

I watch my father filling in Megumi's left eye. I know that eye, its smallness, its Asian teardrop, its engaging brown. He will not confront Paco. He will not confront his wife. They must decide for themselves. I understand. If I discover Megumi watching a man in the Indian restaurant where we often eat lunch, or the little playhouse on a warm night, it hurts. A little knife stabs me in the side. But I will not speak. She must love me in the face of other men.

The singing is louder, comes close. My father cracks the pencil against the floor, then stands and paces. He pushes his fingers through his hair and shakes his head. I grab the stool before it falls, and look at my fiancée.

"We should go," Megumi whispers.

"No, I can't leave him now." I go to the window where he kneels, and peer over the sill with him. I see nothing. The song has stopped. I wonder if we are the only ones who hear it.

"I think she's there," he whispers.

"Impossible," I say and kneel too.

"Help me push this," he says and unlatches the window.

The windows of the studio have not been opened in years. I pry my fingers into the paint and dirt between window and wood and push as the seal cracks, the window slowly opens and warm, wet air flows in and settles against our faces.

"You watch. I'll be right back," he says and rises.

I watch the alley and the darkness of Paco's windows. A white curtain floats up and settles, floats up again. I imagine an entire life beyond the alley and that apartment. A life my father makes in his paintings. I could have chosen to be a painter. Maybe I am. He taught me to draw. He encouraged me. I drew sneakers and the toaster oven and her, even her, when she dressed in long skirts and shawl, the chopsticks in her hair, to teach at the studio or to dance. I didn't know. I fixed her. He was proud. He taught me to draw without looking at the paper. I remember the first time. The old shoes tangled together, the laces, the perspective of one shoe atop another.

No singing. No sound at all. Not even cars on the roads outside, doors, children, music. Nothing. My knees start to ache, but do not move. This is important. Not to see Paco or my mother, but to carry this through for him.

He returns, and between his legs, pointing straight up, a rifle. It has a thin barrel and a metal sight at the tip. "I didn't know you had that," I say.

"Pellet gun. She's gone, Son."

"Gone," I repeat. Not my mother, I realize. The chair where Megumi sat is empty. The light brightens and burns the empty chair. The canvas where he started to paint her looks like it's smoldering in the intense light.

My father pumps the pellet gun angrily. He claps the stock shut, then pumps it again.

"It needs ten pumps to get through that window," he says between breaths.

He sticks the rusty barrel through the window and rests it against the windowsill. He snuggles the stock against his shoulder and cheek, cocks his head, watches. "Tell me if you see them," he says.

"You won't shoot her?" I ask.

He looks at me like he can't believe I would ask the question. He will not shoot her. He is sane. He will shoot Paco.

"I can't see anything," I say.

My father takes deep, heavy breaths, then blows air slowly from his pursed lips. Some practiced routine for shooting, I guess. But the alley is silent. The windows are empty of movement. I'm not sure if anyone is there anymore.

"I'll check around back," he says. Before I can ask him what this means, he's gone, slipping from the room like a young man, agile, on a grave mission.

I watch the alley for a few seconds and wonder if my father will appear wearing fatigues and a mask of black and green. I hear the screen door slam, but no one appears. I stand and try a few numb steps, but my legs are chunks of wood. I walk like Frankenstein, grab the stool, and lean on it. I stretch my legs and feel the size of the canvas in front of me. My legs run beneath it when I'm this close. I see all the grains and imperfections of the undercoating. I see the spaces in the charcoal lines where he's drawn Megumi's faint outline. It's only a human shape. I don't see *her* yet.

I take a pencil and press the tip into the line of her left eye. I imagine her face close to mine. We are in bed and she's laughing. I smell her; feel her breath on my chin. Her soft eyes widen, and she looks at me; I count three freckles.

When I finally look, I'm surprised to see I've ruined what little there was to start. It looks nothing like her. It seems ridiculous to realize I don't know her well. Maybe I never will. I drop the pencil into the tray. I look toward the front windows of the studio to see if the car is still there. Maybe she waited. I realize that one day she will know some furtive craving I will be unable to satisfy. I open the front door, smell turpentine baking in the heat, the vegetable smell of hot vines, dirt, and grass. The car is not there.

ROB: I want to say this about these pieces—all are remarkably well written. You've got the tools, folks. Good writing, very good writing. Why don't you give yourself a moment and refresh your memory about Erich's story. Remember the guidelines in here: if you feel you have something useful to say, great. Keep it focused on the text and let's work from basics first, but you're under no compulsion to speak. On the other hand, I don't want you to take anything I've said to mean "Keep your mouth shut," either. You will often have wonderful, useful things to say. It won't affect your grade either way. So it's up to you.

No one? OK, I'll start.

The story sets up quite beautifully—line to line, it's nicely written. "His hair is fine and light gray, tossed up from thinking with his fingers." That's a fabulous line; And you set the tone of New Orleans beautifully. You must have responded

to Tom Piazza—remember the Brownsville story? You catch
New Orleans—not derivatively, but in a way reminiscent of
that milieu. Your narrator talks about coming into this place
in the Quarter where artists live, and you evoke it vividly.

The father is an artist, and when you have a father artist
and an accountant son, there's at once a discrepancy that suggests the possibility not only for traditional conflict but also
for the prime mover of conflict, yearning. And there's an interesting kind of undercutting of polarity, in that the son met
Megumi along the Bayou at the New Orleans Museum of Art.

But that undercutting, in fact, is just the foreshadowing
of the actual dissipation of any sense of difference in the story.
The son readily understands his father's art—seeks it out, in
fact, with regard to Megumi—and the father in turn seems
quite comfortable with his son and totally accepting of
Megumi as a future daughter-in-law. The only problem is beyond the wall. And it's a shared problem, of sorts, but it remains a problem.

So I've got the yearning deficit here. There is no dynamic
of desire. It's not until pretty late in the story that anybody
thinks to take any action. Once taken, it gets sort of extreme.
As a result, it feels dragged in. When we get to scenes that
might contain heat—that is to say, scenes that involve the
mother from the past, or even in the present—we never see
her. To make anything of the story, you have to believe that
the mother and even his mother being with his father are somehow important to him. But there's no evidence of that, and this
is where the emotional logic of the story breaks down. Before
there's even a serious reference to the mother's flamenco

career—the background of her stage presence, the relationship of the mother and father, the mother dancing next door
with this Paco guy—all of this is done in summary, abstraction, generalization. There isn't a single memory, not a single
scene, not even a peeking through the window. Here these
double shotgun houses sit. The son comes and goes always to
the father, and yet the mother's right there. We have no real
sense of why there's this absence, this division, this gap between son and mother. The past offense seems to be, even from
his point of view, between the mother and the father. It's not
as if he's sided with the father in some drastic way against the
mother. Then when we hear about the mother learning flamenco in Tulane—and this was some time ago, wasn't it—
there's not even a moment of flashback of his seeing her. If
your mother suddenly turns into a flamenco dancer—there's
a lot of potential here, Erich, but there needs to be a moment
when he sees her dance for the first time, at whatever age, im-
pressionably. And a moment when he is compelled to see her
dance now, in the present of the story. When, for example,
he is somehow compelled to carry those flowers from this door-
step to the other and put them where they're supposed to be,
and then look, peek, spy. We want to see his mother dancing
the flamenco, especially with a strange man.

I would not be surprised to find that this is one of those
stories where there was something hot you were looking into,
something dangerous, and you cooled it down, defensively,
before it got onto the page. So much is possible here if, in fact,
a dynamic of real desire got into the story. As it is, the situation represents only a kind of distant problem to the narrator.

Megumi is not really developed as a character, especially in relationship to him. Why is he seeking the painting? There is a reference briefly to a work in which his mother appears in one of his father's paintings, but it's quite incidental; she's lost in a landscape, and the image doesn't become a functioning part of his psyche; it does not tap into his yearning. There just seems to be so much potential in this story. His father had done a portrait of his mother, and now the son wants to bring Megumi here, to recreate in this woman he's about to marry an emblazoned image of the mother—that, for example, would be possible. Development of that kind of interconnection and connection with desire . . .

When we finally come to a statement of how Paco has corrupted a situation that the narrator might wish to be pure, we begin to get a whiff of yearning. The narrator says that "Paco disrupts an already shaky marriage." He finally asserts a feeling about this but, again, it's done abstractly and analytically.

The absence of a relationship between our narrator and Megumi is also reflected in the fact that he's so open in front of her about what's going on next door. It's as if Megumi vanishes from his consciousness—indeed, that's part of the reason she walks away from him. But how much does she realize here? When she whispers, "We should go," it feels like she understands whatever ache he's feeling but, again, this is only vaguely hinted at, not really *there*.

There's a story full of possible yearning here. It's just that you've distanced yourself drastically from that story. I'm left with the question that I put to most of you at this stage, which is: Did the story come from your head? And then, if so, why?

It could be because the story from the get-go was a willed story, a thoughtful story, an idea story; in which case, when you put this thing away go on to something utterly different. Or, given that there's so much potential, was something coming from your unconscious that began this process, but you flinched and distanced yourself (and us) out of some kind of self-protection? In which case, I still say put it away and don't look at it—but do go back to your protagonist, to his father the artist, and his mother the flamenco dancer. There's a rich circumstance, a wonderful setting, a lot of potential here. But the story itself, as written, is disassociated from it. Do you have a sense at this point of which it is, whether the story is hot and you flinched, or whether the story was cool from the start?

Erich: Oh, yeah. Very cool from the start.

ROB: Well, then I'm impressed that you coolly set up so many possibilities.

Jocelyn: I'm curious why you say *Put it on the shelf.* I thought there was a lot of excellent rendering of setting, for instance. That was something very beautiful.

ROB: No matter how much beautiful stuff—we all have to learn this—I know I do—we're all struggling with it—if you write a thing from your head, *everything* in that piece is tainted. Even if you have passages that are beautifully written, brilliantly sensual, and maybe in their beauty and sensuality have actually come from the outer foyer of your unconscious—you don't go back and try to save those passages. Don't say, "OK, I've already got a good description of New Orleans; I'll just stick that in." An art object is organic, and this beautiful rendering of New Orleans may be exactly the wrong beautiful rendering of New Orleans for the object that's going to come out of this place. This make sense to you, Jocelyn?

Jocelyn: It's so hard.

ROB: It's the hardest thing in the world, but it's necessary. You go back and pull something out of one piece and stick it in another and everything is lost. It will just bend the story to fit an external factor. It's the same danger you run with a literal memory. Yes, Kent.

Kent: In the scene in New Orleans where they're walking down the street—say you go back to your trance, maybe there's something about his mother or something like that . . . it won't be rendered the same way. . . .

ROB: It's in the realm of human possibility that the same brilliant sentence may come back and flow right out of your unconscious once again and work perfectly.

Kent: Or you go back into the artist's studio or into . . .

ROB: Oh, absolutely. Scenes, actions, movements—you can redream them. Sure, he brings Megami into the studio and asks his father to paint her. But you might do that *after* a scene in which either he sees hanging in his father's studio or remembers from his childhood a painting of his mother that the father had done, that memory having been rendered moment to moment from his yearning to find a home again, or to reconnect with his parents, or to something lost—if such a scene is already in the story, then the minute he and Megumi walk into that artist's studio—everything will be different than it was in this version. Every detail—all the receptors will be thrumming to something in the piece that isn't there now. However, if you have some brilliant phrase from the previous draft that you're bound to work in, but which was created in a context without these new scenes in which the yearnings are manifest, then you've got a problem. As I say, it's in the realm of human possibility that walking into that studio, the same brilliant sentence may roll out and turn out to be perfect, but not if you go and get it to save it.

Janet: There's a parallel here with Mary Lee Settle's advice about research, where she says: Don't read about the period that you're researching, read *in* the period . . . magazines, memoirs, letters that were written in that period, and take no notes. Because when you come to write the thing, if you've taken notes you think you have to use them, whereas if you've immersed yourself in the period, what you need will come to you.

ROB: Absolutely. The work is an organism. Any external thing that has its own existence, anything outside the creation of the work that insists on getting in, is like a virus. Once it gets into the body, it will eat up everything around it. The organic nature of art is such that within the process everything must be utterly malleable, utterly fluent, so that everything ultimately can be brought together; and if there's anything in there that will not yield, is not open to change, you cannot create the object.

11

"MY IMPOSSIBLES" BY BRANDY T. WILSON

My Impossibles

My mother stood beside me with the shovel in her hand and I stood looking at the ground wishing I had the shovel and that sweat was dripping from my forehead instead of hers. My mother and I seemed to always be flying at different ends of the earth, and whatever I did, she did it better. It was a quarter past four on the Saturday afternoon of my weekend visit and the poles for the garden arch were still in plastic wrap at my foot. I bought the thing for a project my mother and I could do together while I broke the news to her. I had miscarried and she wouldn't be a grandmother after all, and never would be, through me anyway. She delivered and raised three children practically on her own and I couldn't even carry one. It had been a last-ditch effort on my part anyway. My marriage was falling apart and I thought it would mend that as well as change the way my mother saw me. Now my plan was to toil over this structure for my mother's garden and hope she wouldn't see me as the worthless failure of a woman I felt I was. But, as I said, she had the shovel and was about to start digging the holes at the very same instant that I was trying to find the sentence in the instructions that told us we needed to dig holes.

"You gonna move, or am I gonna have to shovel around ya?"

"Just a minute, Mother! I'll do it, just let me see how far apart they're supposed to be." I scanned the page and flipped the instructions over. There was nothing but a diagram on the other side, with no measurements. "You don't know where you want it anyway."

"I know exactly where I want it. So dig the first hole, then we'll see how far apart they need to be." She held out the handle.

I stood up and stuck the shovel into the hard black clay that crumbled into a nearby crack instead of scooping in as I pushed down with my foot.

"Give me that. For God's sake, Becky, don't you know how to shovel?" She yanked it from my hand and dug into the clay. With one swift nudge of her foot, she scooped up a chunk and threw it to the side. She did this two more times. "That oughta be enough. Gimme the pole."

"But, Mom, we've got to measure it."

"All right, get down there and measure it."

I grabbed the tape measure from the tool box and measured from the center of the hole to where I thought the next hole should be. She was grinning when I stood back up. "What?"

"Ain't you gonna measure the width of the arch first or we just gonna dig and hope it all works out?" She held out her hand for the measuring tape and I complied. "Why don't you just sit and watch. You don't need to be out here in the hot sun anyway."

Here was my chance. She brought it up; now I could tell her. But this was not what she meant.

"Becky, did you hear me? At least go in the house and put some sunscreen on if you're gonna just stand there and not get in the shade. This is Texas, you can still get a sunburn after four." She snapped the measuring tape back in and then pulled it out over the pole that connected the front of the arch to the back. I dusted my hands and moped toward the house.

It had always been this way. No matter how hard I tried to live up to the woman my mother was and wanted me to be, I couldn't. This was never more clear to me than when we lived alone together for the first time. At the end of the first summer in the house my mother bought after the divorce, the heat of the summer battles was over and she didn't talk about my father much anymore. We were settled. The furniture was in place, the boxes unpacked, and the yard, the one thing my father would never let my mother spend money on before, was gorgeous. This small rectangular patch of grass was placed directly in front of our porch. I say "placed" because that's just what it was. My mother bought a truckload of grass squares at the local lawn-and-garden center and placed them, like she was playing Tetris, between railroad ties that outlined the flower beds and our house. I had always wanted grass like this and the plush blades tickled my bare feet when on a day that August I took my shoes off just to walk across it.

"Why don't you quit prancin' around on the grass and help me out for a change," my mother muttered without looking from the dirt where she was yanking up weeds. She patted the dirt back down by the wild wisteria bush that she built the bed around. Its long coned bunches of purple flowers bounced around her when she brushed up against them. "Get down here and start pulling out anything that doesn't belong."

I squatted beside her, reached in and wrapped my hand around a long, thick weed sticking up above the rest, and pulled. My hand slid up its stalk and over the sticky seeds at the top. I fell back on my rear, and she started laughing. I scrambled back to my squat.

"You're gonna have to get down on your knees and give it some elbow grease."

"Fine," I said and stood up.

"I didn't think that would last long." She didn't even look up.

"I'm just going in to put on something else, I don't want to get these shorts dirty," I protested and ran into the house. I dug my bathing suit top out of the drawer, slid on my cut-offs, and then checked myself in the bathroom mirror. After pulling my hair back and then readjusting my bangs, I lubed up with some cocoa butter and went to the door.

"Don't stand there with the door wide-open, Becky! How many times do I have to tell you, we can't afford to air-condition the outdoors!" she screamed from her rocking chair. She was finished and had taken up her customary seat on the front porch to smoke. I shut the door and slunk into the chair beside her.

"This ain't the prom, Becky, it's just yard work. I swear, for a sixteen-year-old, you sure don't have much sense." She laughed, her cigarette bobbing up and down on her lips. She had noticed the lipstick I smeared on my lips just before I walked out the door. I snarled. By this time of the summer her hands were rough, her nails were jagged, and she had a farmer tan all the way down to built-in socks and the most awkward stripes across her thighs and back from too many different tops and shorts. Her outfits, as well as the tan lines, were a running joke between us.

"Well, I'm sorry if I don't have any farmer gear," I said, thinking that I couldn't get tan even if I dipped myself in chocolate.

Sweat dripped down her temples, and she grabbed the wet rag off of her shoulder to drag across her entire face and neck. "Well, I guess asshole and that slut he's been seein' ain't gonna drive by and flaunt themselves today," she said and punched out her cigarette in the clay pot filled with sand she kept on the front porch. Then she added with a sarcastic snarl, "And I so wanted him to see my new flower beds. I put them out just for him." My father had driven by the house only once with his new girlfriend since he moved out last October. But with my brothers off at college, the divorce had left us alone and once was enough. I still wanted to kid her about her tan, but I knew that it was too late. It was normal for her to change subjects in the middle of a conversation, especially if it was one I had begun.

When I returned from getting the sunscreen she instructed me to put on, she was already on the third hole for the garden arch. The sun was getting lower, giving a sheen to the handle of the shovel as her sweat dripped past her hands and slid down the slick wood.

"Becky," she wiped the sweat off her forehead with the rag she still kept over her shoulder when doing yard work, "go unwrap those poles and start assembling them for one side, while I finish up these holes."

The poles were white and made of a hard plastic that wouldn't bend even if you ran over them with a truck. I pulled each one out of its individual plastic wrapper and lined them up on the ground: long with long, short with short, curved with curved, then all of the skinny round ones that connected the back to the front. My mother was on the last hole so I skimmed the instructions and began piecing it together by glances at the diagram.

By the time I had one section of the garden arch assembled, Mother was working on her third cigarette, letting it dangle from her lips as she handed me the next pole. I pressed the top pole for the front left side down over the bottom half which had been cinched for the fit. Beads of sweat rolled into my eyes and I grabbed the bottom of my shirt to wipe it away.

"Here," she handed me her rag, "you'll stretch your shirt out."

I took the rag though it was drenched in her sweat already and wouldn't do me much good. I dabbed it across my hairline and gave it back. "Hand me the arched piece, Mama." She hesitated but gave me the long curved piece of hard plastic. She pulled the rag across her face again. My sweat didn't bother her.

As I reached to slide the arched piece onto the long poles, I stepped backward and my right foot went sideways into one of the holes. I fell onto it with all my weight and went down onto my side, the arched piece still in my hand. My ankle throbbed.

"Well, what in the hell did you do that for? You knew the holes were right behind you." She had been watching me.

I didn't cry, but I wanted to. Not because of the pain, though it did hurt, but because I knew that I wasn't going to be able to tell her like this. I knew she would say that I hadn't been careful enough, that I knew there had been a risk of tubal pregnancy, but that if I had been careful about it I wouldn't have lost the chance to ever have children.

I didn't stand right away, but I moved the pieces of the arch to my side. I just sat there and refused to speak as she stood over me looking at my foot. I thought of all the things I could tell her instead of what had really happened: that I decided that I really didn't want children, that Terry had left me and I was upset, that it was the doctor's fault, not mine. Anything but that I got pregnant to save my marriage and prove a point even though my doctor told me to wait until my body was stronger, until the endometriosis was under control, until I was healthier and I had more time and less stress. Anything but that I knew better and did it anyway.

When I was in the third grade my nicest white shirt with fitted Victorian lace sleeves was ruined when I got hit with a rock at school. I had begged to wear it and she had conceded, reluctantly. After it happened my grandmother had to take me to my mother because she was having her hair done. I saw my reflection in the glass door before I went in. My hair was matted at my temple where it had brushed up against the blood. My eyes were swollen from the tears, and the blood that had run down my face and onto my shirt had dried leaving flaky streaks down my cheeks. The blobs on my shirt were darkening to a smeared maroon mass. I rushed past the counter with my head ducked and went down to the stall where my mother was. She didn't see me approach and I had to tug on the shiny black smock, almost unsnapping it, to get her attention. My mother had a look of confusion, concern, and humor all at the same time. "What have you done now? And look at what's happened to that beautiful shirt," she said like she was holding back a laugh.

I could feel my cheeks flush and my face get as red as the dried blood. "Are you OK?" she asked, like it was an afterthought, and I shook my head with more big tears welling up in my eyes. "Well, I guess you're probably gonna need some stitches." She sounded disappointed, like it was something I'd done on purpose.

Finally, I stood up although I knew my ankle was swelling and would be covered by a purple and green pigment in a few hours. I grabbed the arched piece and slid it into its slots.

"You all right?" she asked in the same afterthought way she'd had about my head.

"I'm fine, hand me the hammer, Mama, I'm almost done with this side." I tried to sound excited but it came out more like frustration.

Mother hunched over and yanked at the weeds when she finished the last hole. Her legs were muscular and tan. The veins in her arms bulged from the work. She looked young and strong enough to still have her own babies, but that's when it happened.

She pulled at one more weed and then stopped, but stayed hunched over, and then grabbed her stomach. She didn't say a word but went to her knees and looked up at me in a panic. I dropped the plastic poles at my feet and knelt beside her.

"Mama, what is it? What's wrong?" I reached for her arm.

"I think I'm having female problems," she said with an emphasis on the first syllable of *female*.

"Oh." I hesitated, "I mean, what?" I helped her to her feet and we walked toward the house. Bright red blood had soaked through the seat and part of the leg of her pants. I felt my face go cold and pale.

"My periods have gotten really bad lately," she explained almost out of breath as we reached the door and went inside. "I'm flooding like this all the time. I think I might have to have something done about it." She went into the bathroom and closed the door. "Get me a change of clothes, Becky."

I rummaged through her drawers and found a clean pair of panties and some pants. She cracked the door and I handed them to her. "Get my purse and bring me the cordless phone."

"Do you want me to call someone for you, Mama?" I asked standing outside the door already with the phone.

"No, I've got to call. Just get my purse."

When she came out of the bathroom she still couldn't stand up straight and tears were welling up in her eyes. "Are you sure, Doctor?" she said into the phone. "OK, I'll be there in a few minutes." She hung up and handed the phone back to me. "We've got to go to the hospital, Becky. I may have to have surgery."

"What? Surgery, why?"

"I've been considering having a hysterectomy for a while and with all the trouble I've been having, the doctor thinks we may have waited too long." I grabbed her arm and helped her to the car.

A nurse was hovering just inside the door when I got up to her room that night. "*Shh!* Be quiet now, she's still resting from the surgery." The nurse spoke in a stern whisper that probably would have woken my mother up before any noise that I would have made. I sat down without a reply and pulled at a piece of the plastic fern by the bed. The room was cold and the window small. Stiff gray curtains hung past the frame in an attempt to make it look larger. The TV was off, but the room vibrated with a dull hum. I wanted to leave. The cinder block walls reminded me of a padded cell. The only light on in the room was a reading light above my mother's head and I wondered how she could look so pale and sunken yet swollen at the same time.

My grandmother was reading a romance novel in the chair beside me. On the cover was a woman in a torn white cotton dress with ruffles that hung over one shoulder. Her hair was a stringy blond that flew back from her face with the imaginary wind. She clung to the chest of a large man, almost twice her size, with a furrowed brow and a hand on his hip like he had been playing king of the mountain and won.

"Did it go all right?" I asked in a whisper softer than the nurse's had been.

"They said she'll be fine, no difference between a regular hysterectomy and an emergency one." My grandmother went back to her book while I stared at my mother sleeping.

Weeks after her stitches were removed her scar remained red and it drew up the skin around it. She made a point to show me that they had shaved off all of her pubic hair. She looked bare, stripped. They had sliced vertically, directly down her stomach, and the scar was set deep into her skin with her belly swollen on either side.

"Look at that, from my belly button down to my impossibles," she told me. She was standing in her room holding her nightgown up and looking into the full-length mirror on the door. "Now I've been cut into twice." She turned away from the mirror and dropped her nightgown to tell me this.

This was news to me. I may have been told before but I didn't remember another scar.

"The first time was from when I had you and like to have died. Now I've had two emergency surgeries," she glared over the words like I ought to apologize.

"You almost died from having me? I thought you were so happy that I was a girl and that you didn't even believe them until they put my butt in your face?" This is the story I liked to remember.

She brushed through her hair, straight back, and then scrunched it with her fingers. The brush was still in her hand as she spoke. "I sure enough did make them put your butt in my face. I was so happy to finally have a little girl I couldn't see straight. But afterwards, I had my tubes tied and they didn't hold my stomach."

"Why would they need to do that?"

"I was coughing and they were supposed to hold my stomach so that I didn't rupture any of the stitches. Well they didn't and I came untied and hemorrhaged. They liked to have let me die. I kept telling them that I didn't feel right, that something was wrong. But they didn't listen."

I interrupted. "Why didn't they listen? Couldn't they tell?"

"Well, you'd think so, I was swole up like a toad frog. But they just kept telling me that it was normal to feel that way after having a baby or some such nonsense. I told 'em that I knew just exactly what it was like to have a baby; this was my third. But they still wouldn't listen. Finally when the nurse came in to check my blood pressure I was damn near dead and they had to do emergency surgery."

I crossed my legs under me and sat up higher in the desk chair.

She repeated herself, "I was bleeding to death. Those nurses weren't watchin' me like they were supposed to."

I grabbed my side of the completely assembled arch and lifted while my mother lifted the other side. She was finally able to get out and work in the yard again, but now everything was just about done blooming and it was almost time to get the yard ready for winter. "I want to get that arch in before it gets cold, Becky. That way next year the wisteria will just run up it," she told me. We angled the arch beside the holes, then lifted it in. It slid in with a clunk and one of us had to hold it while the other packed the dirt around the poles. I volunteered for the dirt.

"Get the water hose over here and wet that old clay. It'll harden like concrete around the poles," Mother said, pointing toward the hose cart at the side of the house.

After reattaching the hose to the faucet I wheeled the cart to the flower bed where the arch now stood with my mother's support. The water was cool. When it hit the hard, cracked ground it didn't soak in right away but splashed against my legs.

I shoveled the mud into the holes and knelt down to pack it with drier dirt at the top.

"Now, that's just right," she said and let go of the arch.

The project had been a success. In a year or so the white plastic arch would be dripping with cones of purple petals. But I still hadn't told her.

She was already smoking when I got around to sitting down with her on the porch.

"Mama, I'm sorry if . . . ," I started to say, trying to fight back the tears as they inched into my eyes, but she seemed to have softened a bit. Her body was relaxed against the back of the chair, and she was rocking. "I know I'm not exactly what you expected in a daughter."

She stopped rocking and looked right at me. "Oh honey, yes you are. You're independent, full of life, everything I ever wanted." She leaned back in her chair again and looked out over the yard. "Never mind that silly husband of yours, and doctors can do so much these days; you may have children someday if you want, just look at what all has happened to me. All the problems I'm still alive to tell it."

"No, you don't understand," I protested.

"I know you two aren't getting along. He hasn't called all weekend, not even to see if you got here safe. You don't need him anyway, and you should be grateful for that. It wasn't like that when I got married."

"That's not what I meant. How did you know I lost the baby?" I tried to be pathetic, but it came out hard and cracked.

"It's been three months since you told me you were pregnant. You haven't said much about it since. At first I thought it was because I was sick but you have been completely avoiding the subject. Besides, you're shaped just like me. If you were three months along you'd already be swole up and big all over." She gave a half grin when she said this.

"Mama, I'm never gonna have a baby," I blurted and glared at her.

"Do you really want children? I mean, you have so much more. Just look at me and what all I've had to go through with my body. When I was your age I thought that children, and a husband, was all there was. But you have a choice." She took the last drag of her cigarette and put it out.

I couldn't believe this was the same woman who put me through ballet, piano, tap, and a myriad of other things to try and make me into a lady so I would grow up and marry well, have babies, and repeat.

She leaned back and propped her foot against the porch post. "You probably only did it to prove a point anyway." She laughed.

Instead of crying or screaming, I leaned back in my rocking chair and grabbed one of her cigarettes.

"I just thought a baby would . . ." I stopped to take a long first drag from the cigarette.

"Yeah, that's what we all think at one time or another. Now, I love you kids and I wouldn't have it any other way than having had you. But children won't solve your problems."

Even over the smoke, a floral smell still hung in the sticky air. The garden arch was a brilliant white against the rough black dirt at its base and the green of the wisteria all around it. I thought about the day I miscarried and the cramps that woke me up at six in the morning. For about a week afterward all I could think about was sex, though I neither felt like having sex nor wanted to be anywhere near Terry.

"I think my hormones are out of whack," I said.

"Maybe you're about to go through menopause," she laughed and I laughed with her but it wasn't because it was funny. "I don't guess I will ever have to really go through that," she said with a tone that suggested a change of subject.

I held the cigarette awkwardly between my thumb and my forefinger. "The slugs are bad at my house this year. Slimy old things. I can't stand 'em," I complained.

"Pour salt on 'em. They'll just wither up and go away." When she said this I felt like the Morton Salt Shaker girl, without an umbrella of protection over my head, holding my life in my hands, which was still a reflection of her life. I thought about the store-bought wisteria shriveling in my front yard and decided to ask her for a cutting.

"Sure, they just grow up wild around here. I couldn't tell you how long it's been there." She got up to get the shears. After clipping a small branch with lots of leaves and an un-opened bud, she brought it over to me. "Now, don't say thank you or it'll die."

"Why's that?" I took the cutting and twirled it in my hands.

She shrugged, "Old wives' tale."

ROB: What we need always to be in search of is the way in which a character's yearning is manifested. Stories are driven forward by causality. All plot comes from the character's try-ing to get something, to achieve something, wanting, desir-ing, longing for something. The complications ensue from the drive of those yearnings and the attempt to get around the impediments and difficulties that thwart desire.

In Brandy's story—talking now in this artificial, second-ary way—planting things in a garden could operate as a meta-phor for each of the character's barrenness. But barrenness itself is a *problem;* it does not constitute a yearning. You're on the verge of it here, Brandy, but the story does not yet move to the yearning in a clear and comprehensive way. One diffi-culty is that the building of the garden arch has not yet been made to work with metaphorical logic. Another is that some crucial things are told in flashback.

The narrator Becky feels unappreciated. She believes that her mother has always thought her worthless and in effective. The back story starts on the bottom of the second page and goes on for another two pages, recalling an earlier time in the garden. But the put-down element here, the mother's critiques of Becky, feel too small to have stuck and wounded. I need a scene in the back story to reinforce the hurt.

We miss some important things. The father drives by. That's very briefly dealt with. Again, the mother criticizes Becky, but in trivial ways. The mother's flashback to the hysterectomy does not resonate into Becky's grief over her miscarriage; Becky remains merely an observer here. The moment when the mother realizes that she's sick, that there's something wrong with her femaleness, is not in the story. At the end of the story, once it's clear that the mother knows about the miscarriage—which is therefore not a secret after all—she suddenly transforms; she's tolerant and approving, which feels unearned at that point. And then the story finishes on new terms—the cutting of the wisteria branch—so that the climax happens in sensual terms that do not recompose the story.

Nevertheless I think this story is on the verge. I think it came from something hot in you, and that there's yearning fluttering around the edges. The opening lines are often explanatory in a kind of on-the-nose way. Indeed, the first flashback is very sharp: "No matter how hard I tried to live up to the woman my mother was and wanted me to be . . ."

We have to figure out how to flip the story around, from developed "problems" to a dynamic shape that could come out of those problems. If she has been criticized by her mother all her life, and if she had a miscarriage and cannot have children, and her mother has had a hysterectomy, what is the issue here?

What is the deeper issue? It certainly has to do with the common literary theme, identity. But more specifically, what does it mean to be a woman? What is womanness? The yearning is to understand what it means to be a woman in her life. *I yearn to identify myself, to find my identity as a woman.* The challenge is that she's had a miscarriage, she cannot have children. That's the natural yearning that comes out of the problems you give us.

So we begin in the garden. Now we have to find the connection between what she's doing in that garden—the deep, sensual patterned connection between that and this yearning. Again, I'm talking in analytical terms, figuring this out rationally, saying that certain scenes are needed and so forth. It's not the right way to work. But for the moment it's OK, because this is a learning process, and identifying what's needed, going through those motions, is helpful.

What is it in the arch they're erecting in the garden that relates to the yearning I've described? A portal is an opening, which is the female pattern, so there's a suggestion of the female body. (That may not be your intention, but it is a traditional metaphor, so you need to be aware of it. I'm doing this to help everyone understand how yearning relates to what usually ends up in stories; I'm not suggesting this as a way for you to work.) This garden has been cultivated since the departure of the ex-husband, an act of the two women in contradiction to the man. The ex-husband forbade the garden. The male thing was corn and soybeans—I don't know—but this is the thing that the women have done as an assertion of themselves. These things must somehow be in the story in real time.

Perhaps the instructions should say that the placement of the arch is of crucial aesthetic importance, and Becky keeps looking for where to put it? At the moment there's no such suggestion in the instructions. Say the present action has to do with where the arch should go; we know it's important, but we don't know where it goes. She's got this terrible thing to tell her mother. There's a reference made to the ex-husband having driven by sometime in the past. This is an opportunity. Is there a scene there?—I don't know—but think in terms of what's in front of you.

Or suppose we see the moment when the mother becomes sick. The mother's female body is still intact, and the daughter doesn't know how to approach her with bad news. Maybe she approaches her, and the mother's horrified—but in any case let the event of the mother getting sick and going to the hospital be in the story. She has an emergency hysterectomy and then the mother and the daughter are on the same plane. The mother always criticizes the daughter about what it means to be a woman—so that strain between them is indeed about what this means, and we dramatize the reality of Becky's fear of confessing her miscarriage.

Then, what happens in the hospital room between mother and daughter where the mother has just had her womb removed? There's a lot that's still to be dreamed here. Maybe in the dreaming you will have had her tell the mother already, and she had a harsh reaction, so that there will be a reconciliation. Or maybe this is when she tells her—even as the mother's devastated—*this is something as women we can share because I've lost a child.* Suddenly there's a very complex relationship possible, and a complex reaction involved.

Whether we come back to putting the arch in at the end of the story I don't know. I'm sketching out a way in which the stuff that's in the story can be transformed from problem to yearning, and the way that yearning can find its arc; a way that everything can be pulled together, so that mother and daughter together redefine what it means to be a woman. I hate the way I'm talking here. You understand why I'm doing it, right? Feel free to alter or ignore anything I've said. But that's the *kind* of thing all stories need in order to shine in their best light. There's a lot of good stuff here, Brandy, and I think it'll be a wonderful story. It's just a matter of taking the problems and transforming them toward the dynamic that will make us understand what's at stake.

Jocelyn: You mentioned "metaphorical logic." How does logic come to bear on this, or is there any need for logic?

ROB: *Logic* itself is being used here in a metaphorical way. I mean that a story has emotional logic; there's a spiritual logic, an aesthetic logic to a work. The universal principle behind any narrative sequence is the yearning. But once the character's desires are driving her forward, then, given that yearning, given that character's ability, her circumstances, the milieu, the kinds of obstacles challenging her, there is a logic of sorts to what goes in and what stays out—what scenes are necessary, inevitable, emotionally logical, and what sense details are the logical choices.

The logic here is not that of rational premises and intellectually perceived results but rather a kind of emotional, psychological, aesthetic, spiritual, metaphorical fitness. If certain conditions exist and they are accessed by the writer through the senses and the dreamspace and perceived by the readers through their senses and their dreamspace, certain things will necessarily follow. That describes the kind of logical form. It's an emotional logic.

Janet: I have heard you, including in these lectures, talk about the way that you picked up images, and I know that when I read you one of my great pleasures is seeing the repetition of motif. There are many other writers' works where I'm not aware of that as a pleasure; mostly I'm reading for the page-turning, wanting to know what's going to happen. As a *writer* my main pleasure is that other sort, and it comes at the moment when a metaphor or motif clicks into place.

ROB: Let me address the "logic of the metaphor." Metaphor works, of course, at its first level as a vivid intensifier of sensual experience, to enhance sensual access to the creative world. It vivifies the moment. That's its first function. But metaphor then has, like all the other sensual elements in this organically whole object, a pattern behind its content. Whether you think of it as motif from the reader's point of view, or think of it as recomposing, reincorporating things that are already at play in the work, the metaphor's essential pattern needs to intersect or interlock with the pattern echoed microcosmically and macrocosmically in the work. The movement between one metaphor and another is also by its pattern the arc of the character through the book.

12

"MY SUMMER IN VULCAN" BY RITA MAE REESE

My Summer in Vulcan

When I open the door, Paul is standing at the top of the stairs grinning, with one hand behind his back. He looks past me and puts a finger to his lips, pulling his other hand from behind his back, revealing a bouquet of flowers. I notice some red and orange and yellow before he winds his hand behind his back again. He's wearing a blue sports coat though it's hot outside and too-white running shoes. He steps through the doorway.

"Hello, Lilly," he says.

"Sheila's in the living room, playing with the baby," I tell him.

I was getting the baby dressed to go when Sheila, that's my sister, started tickling Gracie and acting goofy. Gracie's the baby; Sheila's her mom. People say Gracie looks more like me.

I sit down at the kitchen table to put my tennis shoes on. They are looking pretty ratty. Last time I talked with my mom I told her I needed a new pair but she hasn't sent the money yet. We'll see. I can hear Paul and Sheila laughing the goofy grown-up-for-babies laugh and then the quiet murmuring sounds they make when they kiss. I bet Sheila hasn't finished putting Gracie's shoes on yet and sure enough, when I walk in, the baby is waving her socked feet around in the air, looking up at Paul and Sheila kissing. Sheila has the bouquet in one hand and walks past me into the kitchen, sighing something about water and avoiding my eyes. Paul looks directly into mine, grinning purposefully. His eyes are a watery blue, like shallow water.

"Isn't she beautiful?" he asks me.

She is. She has long silky brown hair that I used to brush and brush. I thought it would be more like that, staying with her this summer. Today she has her hair pulled back and she's wearing a white sundress with eyelets and daisies embroidered in white from the waist up and with little white buttons all the way up the front. She has always been beautiful. I just shrug.

"And she's got a fine ass."

"Shut up, Paul," my sister warns him from the kitchen over the sound of running water.

I sit on the couch, capturing one of Gracie's feet at a time and screwing the little sneakers down onto each. She captures the first sneakered foot and watches me.

"It's good for her to know about loving. Not like . . ."

I don't look up but I can hear his voice travel into the kitchen, the words now pitched in their special frequency, his and Sheila's, and indiscernible from this distance.

I wonder if he has just said her husband's name. We never say it on these Tuesday and Thursday afternoons while he's at work and Paul, Sheila's instructor from the community college, comes over. Jack, Sheila's husband, simply ceases to exist for those hours and I wonder what will happen when he becomes real again. I wonder if any of us will cease to exist that same way some day.

I hoist the baby up on my hip and she bats at my cheek. She smells like baby, like fresh bread but powdery. Her hands are sticky but I don't want to stop to wash them.

I'm halfway down the stairs and nearly outside when Paul calls for me to hold up. He gives me five dollars in case I decide I want anything. He squeezes the baby's cheek with one of his square hands. "Be a good girl," he says.

I've only been in Vulcan a few weeks but I've covered every inch of this town, not that there are that many inches of it to cover. It's bigger than where me and my sister grew up—Wolf Pen, West Virginia, which isn't even on a map, or not on one I've ever seen; there's about fifty families, a stoplight, and a gas station, nothing else. Wolf Pen is 136 miles from Vulcan but Sheila acts like it's in another hemisphere. Since she's moved here a year ago she has come home three times, the last time to pick me up and bring me here to help with the baby for the summer.

In Vulcan, there's a glass-blowing plant at the far west end, about a mile past anything else on Highway 20. There is a library, and a police station, and some shops downtown that sell candles and knickknacks. My favorite shop is Aunt Dee's Quilts. The sign in the window says that the quilts are hand-stitched and inside it always smells like apple pies, so much so

that I expected Aunt Dee to offer someone, me or one of the
rare customers, a slice. I finally figured out the smell was coming from the potpourri burners on the little table at the back,
where she sold some picture frames and candles. Aunt Dee
doesn't offer me anything. She was nice to me the first time I
came in, cooing over Gracie, but after that she watched me
like I might try to stuff one of the quilts up my T-shirt or pull
out a can of black spray paint and start running up and down
the aisles turning all of her pretty quilts black.

The quilts are pretty and Gracie and I like to go in if
Sophia is working instead of her stepmother. Sophia is three
years older than me and goes to the same school Sheila goes
to. She's a little fat and never wears shorts, even when it's over
ninety degrees outside, like today. She always wears T-shirts
with the names of bands I've never heard of and her hair always seems greasy. But she's nice and I think she's smart but
it's kind of hard to tell.

Gracie and I like to look at all of the nice colors in all of
the pretty patterns; my favorite is a double wedding ring mostly
in blues. My sister is supposed to pay me for babysitting at the
end of the summer, and I'm going to take that money, it'll be
just enough, and buy that quilt. I always look to make sure it's
still there.

I like to pretend I'm shopping for my own home. When
I get older I'll have a beautiful home and Gracie will come
over in the afternoons when she's a teenager like I am now
and ask me for advice and tell me about how she can't get along
with her mom and I'll listen but of course I won't say a word
against my sister. Gracie won't talk about killing herself be-

cause she'll know she always has my house to come to and me
to listen to her. She's smart and she'll know that's enough. In
the quilt store Gracie pats her hand against the air, wanting
to feel the fabric like I do but I won't let her. I don't let her
drool or get anything on the quilts.

Sophia is working today so we go in. She's reading a
book behind the counter. I park Gracie's stroller and sit on
the stool beside Sophia. She keeps reading her book. I watch
a woman in jean shorts and with dark wavy hair pulled back
in a ponytail running her fingers lightly over the fabrics. I
sit up higher on my stool so I can see her long bare legs. The
wood floor creaks beneath her feet as she weaves between a
dark blue quilt with tiny yellow flowers in a starburst pattern and the crazy quilt, this king-size riot of reds and oranges
and yellows, with gold and shiny strips and silk and velvet,
like a costume I'd seen once in a school play—the guy was
an old poet or something and would just come onstage and
say outrageous things and then be gone. The other characters never really talked to him, not even to tell him to shut
up, mind his own business; I didn't get it.

She comes up to the counter and tells Sophia that she
wants the crazy quilt and Sophia goes over with a ladder to
pull it down from the rod that hangs from the ceiling. The
woman watches her for a minute. I can smell her perfume over
the apple pie smell. She smells golden. I make myself busy
getting the squirming Gracie out of her stroller and trying to
get her to play with one of her plastic books or the ring of big
plastic keys. The woman smiles at us but I pretend not to see
her. Sophia calls me over to help her fold up the quilt and I

start to put Gracie back in the stroller but the woman asks if she can hold her. She coos and bounces Gracie while Sophia and I struggle to fold the quilt down into a manageable size. Sophia makes faces at me while we stand across from each other, bringing our hands together and then apart, the quilt growing smaller each time.

The woman hands me back the baby, telling me that I have a beautiful daughter. I don't correct her. When she's gone, I tell Sophia I'm going to miss that quilt. Sophia motions for me to follow her to the door of the back room. She flings the door open dramatically and I see boxes stacked five feet high with quilts just like the ones hanging up front perched in plastic on top of each. Even the crazy quilt has boxes and boxes of more just like it. I say, "I thought they were hand-stitched," and Sophia says, "Yeah, in Pakistan," when she shuts the door.

"Why didn't you just get one out of the back then?"

"She wouldn't even want it then, dummy."

Gracie starts crying in her stroller, kicking her feet furiously. She doesn't like for me to be out of her sight for even a minute. I pick her up and quiet her down while Sophia goes back to reading her book. I tell her we've got to go and she just grunts, waves a little without looking up when we're going out the door.

Gracie is looking around like she's lost something and won't stop crying. I put the pacifier in her mouth and she spits it out. Sometimes I think it would be a lot easier if I just had to stay gone for a few hours but without the baby. Sometimes I picture leaving Gracie on one of the benches in the town square and finding her in the exact same spot, two hours later, still sleeping. It'd be nice to have a locker to put her in where she'd be safe and a pause button so she wouldn't get scared or bored.

We pass the pharmacy. A woman walking out looks at me like I've been beating the baby to make her cry. I stop outside the pharmacy window and pull Gracie up out of her stroller. *Shut up*, I hiss in her ear. She looks at me for a second from her wet, red face and stops, like she understands me and then she starts in again louder, bouncing her body like she can bounce away. I pinch her calf. *I ought to stuff you in a trash can*, I whisper. She slumps against me, cries against my shoulder like she's lost her last friend. I feel bad. I relax my grip, hold her gently and say *Gracie, Gracie, Gracie* over and over in her ear, as soft as I can.

She stops crying, drawing a few sharp breaths after the tears stop. I look into the pharmacy, through all of the posters and displays. The only person in there is the woman behind the counter. I've already read all of the cards in there. I imagine buying one, "Thinking of you," for my mom. But it seems like a lie. I think about buying one for Sheila, "For a GREAT! sister," but she's not great anymore. Maybe it would guilt her into being at least a good sister again.

I take Gracie into the library, which is the best place as long as she's quiet. If I let her taste the books she doesn't cry. We stay in the back aisles and I rotate the books in her hands so none of them get too soggy. She drops them a lot and it used to make me mad. All of the people here are nice. I got a library card last week so I check out some fairy tales for the baby and a book called *Zami* for me. The cover is orange and has a woman standing between an island and a city. I look at Sheila's watch: 4:00, too early to go back but I'm tired. I want to go home.

When we get back, Paul's station wagon is still there. It's unlocked. I think about putting Gracie in the backseat. She's falling asleep. I've put the books in the dirty blue canvas seat of the stroller and I'm carrying her; she's still cranky and her face starts to ball up when I try to put her down. Her little body is hot and sticky and heavy. I could sit in there with her and read or just lock the doors and go for a walk by myself. I'm not sure I want to go upstairs now. What are they doing?

The baby sighs. She doesn't know we're almost home. I have a key. I park the stroller, leaving the books at the foot of the stairs. I grab the diaper bag from the back and walk quietly up the stairs. Gracie starts to whimper but I hush her. Maybe they're in the bedroom and we can just sneak in. I open the door and tiptoe in, glancing to the left. I can see down the hallway just far enough to see the bedroom door is closed. I put the diaper bag on the kitchen table and Gracie starts crying again.

They're in the living room, on the floor, but it's dark in there so I can't see if they are dressed or not. Gracie is really wailing now and I take her and put her in her crib, try to give her a bottle which she knocks away from her face. I keep saying *sssh* but she won't even look at me, her eyes are sweeping over the room like a searchlight.

"What's wrong with her?" My sister is suddenly there, picking up the baby who is hiccupy from all of her crying.

I almost say she wants her mother, because that's the first thing I think and the first time it's occurred to me. But I don't want to admit it.

"I think she's got a fever."

Sheila starts pacing slowly up and down the room, running her hand against Gracie's forehead, bouncing her. Gracie is quieting.

I go into the living room and Paul is sitting on the couch, reading one of Jack's magazines. He looks up at me.

"Come here and talk to me," he pats the sofa beside him. I sit in the chair next to the sofa, look out the window behind him.

"Did you have fun?" he asks and I wonder if he expects me to ask him the same question. I shrug. He looks at my face.

"So, you're sixteen, huh? Sheila tells me you're sixteen."

I look down at the floor but remember they were just there, doing something I don't want to think about now.

"You and I should get to know each other, spend some time alone together. Sheila talks a lot about you," he says, moving closer to my chair.

I look at him. Why do I think he's lying? His Sheila doesn't even know me, maybe that's why.

"I want to get to know Lilly, the woman of mystery and babysitter extraordinaire," he is leaning on the arm of the sofa, whispering and smiling like he's telling me some great news.

"Sure," I say.

"What do you want?" he asks.

"What are you talking about?"

"You know, what do you want out of life?"

"Oh, what do I want to be when I grow up?" This is the question adults love to ask, like they're taking a survey.

"No. No one ever knows that and even if they do, who cares? What do you want now? What does Lilly want, right now?" he pokes his finger at my chest, a few inches away. I pull my shoulders in tighter.

I shrug. "Everybody wants something," he says.

I wonder when my sister is coming back in. I can hear her singing to the baby.

"Why do you want to know?" I decide I don't have to be as nice to him as I am to regular adults.

"If you find out what somebody wants, you know who they really are. I just want to know you."

"What do you want?"

"I just told you: to know you."

"You know my sister."

"Lilly has claws. Good for her. Come on, Lilly, if you had three wishes, what would they be?"

Wishes? Is this what he teaches at his community college?

"World peace."

"Come on, that's a cop-out."

"There's nothing wrong with world peace," I say, sitting up straighter. He's somehow honeyed his voice so that the words seem smooth and inevitable.

"Boring."

"I'd wish for everyone to be happy, including me." I know I don't want to be unhappy but I haven't given much thought to the alternative.

"You're a regular fucking Girl Scout, aren't you?"

"If everyone isn't happy and you are, then they have a reason to want to make you unhappy. The only way to guarantee you can stay happy is to make sure everyone else is." I'm making this up as I go along but it makes sense to me. I like it.

"No one stays happy, Lilly." He puts his hand over mine on the arm of the chair, like he's consoling me. I just look at it.

He leans closer and says, his voice thick now, "You're a virgin, aren't you?"

I get up and lock myself in the bathroom. My sister hasn't gotten into the bathroom for a shower yet. She's in her bedroom. She always showers after Paul. Sometimes when I get back she has already showered, sitting around the living room in her robe with her hair still damp, smoking and listening to the same albums she listened to when she still lived at home.

I take off my clothes and leave them in a pile on the floor. I look at myself in the medicine cabinet mirror. I can hear them saying good-bye to each other. It takes a long time. I wish there were a full-length mirror in here but the only one in the apartment is in Sheila and Jack's bedroom and they don't really like it when I go in there. Or worse, they think it's funny when I look at myself for too long, or Jack does anyway.

Sheila pounds on the door. "Let me in. I need to take a shower," she yells.

"I'm in the tub," I call out sweetly.

"Well get out!"

"Don't you need to be fixing Jack's dinner anyway?"

She hits the door again hard but goes away.

In this mirror I can see down to my waist. Once I took the little stepladder in with me and stood on it in front of the mirror.

I could see almost all of the way down to my knees and it looked like a painting, or something someone *should* paint. But Jack saw me taking the ladder out of the bathroom and kept asking me what I was doing with it.

I don't like my face so much but I like my body though I know girls my age aren't supposed to. My face is a little too sharp, wolfish in the wrong light and bad pictures, pale with always at least two pimples at any one time, like there's a demon beneath my skin with a pimple quota. My lips are like Sheila's but without lipstick it isn't all that noticeable really. My chin is a little pointier, my nose a little bigger. And my eyes aren't brown like hers, soft like a puppy's or something. My eyes are not any color really, sort of gray, sort of blue, sometimes kind of green, a little gold. One day a tall girl all in black in the lunch line stared at my face and then started saying real loud, "Your eyes is two different colors. That's creepy. Look, look, Charlene. One's blue and one's green." They peered into my face and I didn't know what to do so I just stood there. "You must be the devil or something," she concluded. After I finished my lunch I went into the girl's bathroom and put my face close to the mirror.

I like my ribs, just a faint ripple under the skin, the belly and the belly button (which isn't a button at all, more like a little tunnel and I imagine it going clear through me so that if I stood outside naked I could feel a breeze blow all of the way through my center), my breasts which my hands can cover completely when I want them to, my collarbone, my shoulders, my arms which I position to look like women in paintings or pictures. I pretend I'm an artist's model and hold a pose for a valiantly long time.

I run hot water in the tub and put one of Sheila's red bath oil beads in the water, watch the skin of the ball peel away and the oil creep out like timid schoolchildren. I lower my body slowly into the hot water, having to let my skin get used to the heat. I take the wash cloth and cover my pubic hair, the edges of the square of yellow fabric almost touching my hip bones. I relax my body and the cloth drifts away.

I used to sit in the bathroom with Sheila while she took a bath, before she moved out of Mom's house. Sometimes I'd even wash her back for her. She'd tell me about the people at her school, Stonewall Jackson High School, where I'd go too one day. She'd tell me who said what, who liked who, who wore what, who was getting fat (and that ugly girls got fat and the pretty girls got pregnant).

I raise up my wrist. I'd forgotten to take off Sheila's watch. I unclasp the silver buckle of the black band and lean over to put it on the toilet lid. I used to borrow Sheila's stuff all the time; I loved wearing her clothes, her jewelry, her makeup. I don't like wearing her watch now. My wrist has a pasty white indent around it from where I strapped the watch on too tight.

Sometimes my sister would sit in the bathtub and cry. She would let me stay sometimes or she'd yell at me, tell me to get out, and call me names. One night, just after she'd started eleventh grade and I'd started sixth, I sat on the toilet lid talking and talking, telling my sister what my teacher Mrs. Cline had said about my art project, and about this girl I couldn't stand. The little window high over the tub was open because it was still warm out, and I could hear crickets. My sister just sat in the water, staring at the dripping faucet.

"Nobody gives a shit," she finally muttered. It hurt my feelings. I stopped talking and looked at her. Her long brown hair was wet and draped over her pale, freckled shoulders and back. I could see two big bright pimples in the field of freckles on her cheek and a row of blackheads on her nose. She drew her knees up to her chest.

"Quit looking at me, you fucking freak." She said it slowly and didn't even turn to look at me.

"What'd I do?"

"Everyone's all caught up in their own stupid shit. You talk and talk and talk about fucking nothing. Just like everyone else. No one cares about any of that shit." She put her head down on her knees and her body trembled, causing a tremor in the water. I could hear her muttering "nobody fucking cares" over and over. I stood up and started to pat her back but I was afraid to.

She lifted her head and snarled, "Get out!" and splashed water at me, soaking the bottom of my pants and the floor and her pile of clothes.

I hold my own arm straight up into the air and watch drops of water glide down it. I can hear my sister singing along with Marvin Gaye. I bring my arm down, clench that hand into a fist. It causes a dent behind the blue strokes of veins leading into the palm. Veins carry blood to the heart, and arteries carry blood away from the heart: I like knowing that. Sheila's knock on the door makes me jump.

                              *   *   *

When I get to the table, Sheila, Gracie, and Jack are already
there. And the flowers that Paul brought are in the middle of
the table. I feel hot, trapped. Has Sheila decided to come clean?
The baby looks fine now and is patting the tray of her high
chair and saying, "Annnh." Jack is spooning mashed potatoes
onto his plate.

     "You drown in there?" Jack asks.

     Sheila jumps up. "I forgot the butter."

     Jack strokes his beard twice, which he always does be-
fore he takes the first bite, three times at the end of the meal.

     "Were you in there primping for your boyfriend?" He
smiles across at me. I can only see half of his face because of
the flowers. I notice the one red rose. The baby stops patting and regards me too.

     I shrug. "No," I say like I'm guessing.

     "Sheila's told me all about it."

     "What?" I get busy putting meatloaf, mashed potatoes,
and peas on my plate.

     "About Paul," he drags the name out, making it two
syllables.

     Sheila puts the butter on the table and sits down. I look
to her for direction but she won't meet my eyes.

     "Your new boyfriend, Paul," Jack prompts. "The poor
bastard brings you flowers and you forget him the same day,"
Jack laughs. "Fickle must run in this family." He leans and
reaches for Sheila under the table. She just scowls and pulls
away.

     "Paul," I say and nod down at my plate.

"When do I get to meet him?" Jack asks, talking before he's completely finished chewing. I'm glad the flowers are obstructing my view of him. And his of me.

"I dunno. I think I can do better." I glance over at Sheila to see if she'll react. She doesn't.

"Well, aren't you something?" He looks over at Sheila, sniffs the air like a dog, grinning. "Are you wearing a new perfume?"

"No. It's the same kind I always wear." She won't look up at him.

He actually gets up and kisses her. She tilts her head away so he gets mostly cheek. He thinks the perfume is for him, which in a way it is, and the clean sheets, the clean floors, the vacant smiles.

He sits down, smiling. "You're too young to be serious about anyone anyway," he tells me. "There's plenty of time for marriage and babies when you grow up."

I spoon in another mouthful of mashed potatoes. They are lumpy and bland; my sister is an awful cook. Gracie starts opening and closing her mouth, watching my spoon. I reach over and spoon a tiny lump of the white paste into her mouth. She makes cooing noises around it.

"Paul's only after one thing," I say as clearly as I can. I feel like I'm in a school play.

Sheila gets up and turns the music up. "How was work?" she asks Jack.

"Fine," he smiles over at her. His job and coworkers are the bulk of the conversations at dinner every night. He looks over at me, dropping the smile. "What makes you say that?"

"Oh, you can tell. Any woman can tell that when a guy's only looking to get in your pants." I sit up straighter in my chair, toss my hair back over my shoulder.

"Sheila, I thought you said this Paul was a nice boy."

Sheila just glares at her plate. I spoon some peas into Gracie's mouth.

"Today he grabbed my titties. I told him to leave."

"Lilly," he says my name sharply and pauses like he doesn't know what to say next. "We don't need to have that kind of talk at the dinner table, young lady. Next time he comes around, you call me. I'll set him straight." He puffs up his chest and squares his shoulders like Paul might be looking in the window.

I nod.

"Idddy," Gracie says, letting some half-chewed peas fall to the tray where she smashes them with her palms. "Iddy Diddy Diddy Diddy."

"What is she saying?" he looks over at Sheila.

"Sounds like Daddy."

She's trying to say my name and they know it but I don't say anything.

Jack reaches over and ruffles her wispy hair. "Are you Daddy's girl?" He gets up and plucks her out of the highchair. He starts dancing her around the kitchen. She grabs his beard with both hands and watches his face, then she starts patting his cheeks as they dance around the table.

"You're too good for him," I stage whisper to Sheila, meaning Paul. "I'm not taking the baby out anymore. I'm staying here. We don't need him."

She looks up from her plate at her husband dancing around, holding the baby over his head now. She still won't look at me. She bursts into tears, scrapes her chair against the hard clean floor, leaves the table without a word to me.

ROB: I want to start by saying something about the coming-of-age story or novel, and in general about child narrators and children as central characters. Such narratives present a particular problem, because we're trapped in the child and she isn't old enough to have any other yearning than: *What's next in this process of growing up? I've got to get out of childhood.*

I don't know the details of your life, or any twenty-two-year-old's life. It's very possible that through your childhood and your adolescence—periods when we are driven by our senses—many of you have gone through serious stresses and turmoil. Some of those intense experiences are the generic struggles of young people, and it may be hard to get past the surface track of those struggles and down to the source of your serious ambition as an artist. That applies to all of us at some point. I came back from Vietnam when I had just turned twenty-seven, and wrote the terrible story you've all heard. Clearly, my unconscious was not ready to be accessed. If I had known the things I'm telling you, I would not yet have looked to Vietnam for my material.

There are no child prodigies in literature—there is no Mozart of fiction—and the great writers, at age twenty-two, are not going to have the vision of the world, or the emotional readiness, or the developed unconscious that they will have at thirty, forty, fifty, sixty, or ninety. That's exciting for you; you've got a lot ahead of you. I just urge you to be patient with yourself. Try to work within the range you will chafe at, because it will feel narrow to you; but work within that relatively narrow range of your artistic authenticity, the intimations that are no longer therapeutic and no longer literal but are tapping into something that no one shares. Be patient with yourself and work through that part of your dreamspace.

I know you're all sitting here with your copy of Rita's story, saying, "Oh shit! Don't tell me this one didn't work!"

This works. It's a wonderful story, Rita. The yearning is really rooted in the central character's situation. This is one of those coming-of-age stories, which does limit you somewhat, but within that range you do it beautifully. You have created little moments that let us know Lilly's identity is involved—a larger identity than "I've got to get out of childhood; I've got to get through a tough family situation"—both problems she has. You have in fresh ways manifested those problems in fine moments of action, and that's a rare thing.

When the story opens we understand almost immediately that this is about identity. Paul stands there grinning with the flowers behind his back, and our first assumption is that he's come for the narrator, Lilly. We do not feel cheated, however, when we realize he's here for someone else; that moment of confusion sets up for us exactly what's going to happen. Paul does—beautiful irony here—put the make on her, and the irony is repeated and twisted at the end, where her sister invents the story of Paul being Lilly's boyfriend. So beginning, middle, and end are tied up brilliantly in that way.

And the issue of identity recurs, recomposes. "I was getting the baby dressed to go when Sheila . . ." Again, we don't realize at first that it's not Lilly's baby, and then we do. *Oh, it's her baby.* Then we find that Lilly is covering for the sister, Sheila, who's fucking her boyfriend behind her husband's back, and Lilly is taking care of the child in ways her sister doesn't. Paul follows Sheila, commenting on her beauty and her ass, and Lilly just shrugs. Sheila's always been beautiful. Then come the wonderful scenes in which Lilly examines her own body, carrying a stepladder into the bathroom and looking in the mirror, and we see she has quite a different kind of body from Sheila's. We already know that she has compared herself unfavorably to Sheila, and also that she used to borrow Sheila's clothes—pretending to be Sheila, maybe? And the baby looks like Lilly. She's having to be mother to the baby, and the boyfriend's after her, and yet she's not what she feels Sheila is. These are wonderful issues of identity.

Rita's poetic sense is quite clear here too. When you're really working well, a single word choice can reveal your motif. "And I sit on the couch, capturing one of Gracie's feet at a time"—brilliant verb—"and screwing the little sneakers down onto each"—another great verb.

Notice that Lilly likes to "pretend I'm shopping for my own home. . . . I'll have a beautiful home and Gracie will come over in the afternoons when she's a teenager like I am now and ask me for advice and tell me about how she can't get along with her mom and I'll listen but of course I won't say a word against my sister." That complexity of relationship is fabulous. "Gracie won't talk about killing herself because she'll know she always has my house to come to and me to listen to her." How many writers of less serious talent would try to get at Lilly's dark side in some direct way—"Oh, I feel like killing myself sometimes," blah blah blah—but we know she's talking about herself here. Who else would she be talking about? Why otherwise would she want her own place to be a refuge for Gracie? We know that she's talking about her own distress, and at the same time the lines subtly convey Lilly's personal strength. These abstractions I'm using are woefully inadequate.

There's subtext in all the dialogue. There's not a line of dialogue that isn't working on more than one level. Here's a good montage for you: "He leans closer and says, his voice thick now, 'You're a virgin, aren't you?'" How many inexperienced writers would follow that line with: "Oh . . ." and whatever reactions she has to follow. But here it's "I get up and lock myself up in the bathroom." Cut.

Plot too plays itself out subtly, deftly. Because of Paul's line, Lilly locks herself in the bathroom, which means Sheila can't take her shower, so she douses herself with perfume, and feels compelled to make up a story about the flowers, and now Lilly has the confidence to take advantage of that, and so forth. It all fits beautifully together.

Consider the flashback with Lilly sitting in the bathroom while Sheila's in the tub. Again, it's all about bodies. Sheila's just ripping into Lilly for talking small talk. ". . . stupid shit. You talk and talk and talk about fucking nothing. Just like everyone else." It's a vivid, unexpected moment, and that scene ends in the present time in the tub when Lilly looks at

her own hand in this clinically close way, again pulling it back
to a consciousness of her own self, an identity in her own body.

And yet again: evoking identity in a weird transposition
of roles—Gracie is saying, "Iddy Diddy Diddy Diddy" and Jack
and Sheila try to convince themselves that she's trying to say
"Daddy," whereas we all know that she's trying to say "Lilly."
A brilliant stroke, consistent with yearning as the center of
gravity for this story.

I do have a problem with the very ending. The story does
not resolve itself in the terms it's been set up in. This is really
about who Lilly is, not about who Sheila is. And we have this
little burst of abstract, very reductive analysis that she hands
over to Sheila. The gesture, "I'm not going to play this fucking
game anymore," is fine, but the abrupt assertion of the reason
is not really the core of the story.

The last paragraph offers a lovely tableau, which might
work with some other preparation, but—I'm not sure here. You
need to let go of it and it'll come back if it needs to. The problem is in the penultimate paragraph. The narrator says,
"'You're too good for him,' I stage whisper to Sheila, meaning
Paul. 'I'm not taking the baby out anymore. I'm staying here.
We don't need him.'" I don't feel the irony there. We need to
get to it much more simply, maybe as simply as having Lilly
lean down to Sheila and whisper, "I'm not taking Gracie anymore." I honestly think the fewer words the better. The rest
of it is so beautifully indirect.

Don't get freaked by it, just work it out. Redream the
ending and see if there's some other way. What I need, even
if it's revealed in retrospect, is a sense of the moment in which

she makes this decision. As it stands, I believe the decision, but looking back to see when she made it, I must go all the way back to the beginning of the scene. Even if she doesn't say, "You're too good for him," that's essentially the decision she has made, to be her own person, to dissociate herself from Sheila in this way. But the moment when this decision was actually made—it happened offstage somewhere. It's not just a matter of thinking Paul's an asshole and having an opportunity to say so to Sheila in this ironic, public way. It's more important than that, it has to do with her identity, so we also need a moment in which the decision is made. And indeed, such a decision, the simpler you make it, the more complex it becomes.

All the beats have to be there. This is where craft comes in. Once you get into your unconscious and are working from there, then you need to be sensitive to the rhythm of how things play out, the emotional logic, if you will. And at the end of this wonderful story, there's a step in the emotional logic that has been left out.

Rita: I had a lot of trouble with the first scene because I kept trying to put everything out of my head that I wanted to get into it, just let it go and let it come to me . . .

ROB: You know, that's a lesson of the universe . . . I call it sumo zen—did I tell you I'm a big sumo wrestling fan? I've got a second satellite just so I can get the sumo tournaments from TV Japan. And when the sumo wrestlers are interviewed, they always say the same thing—they barely move their lips— no matter what they're asked, it all boils down to "I'm going to do my brand of sumo, and I'm going to do my best." That's it, folks. That's the lesson of the universe. You do your brand of sumo, and you do your best. And implicit in that concept is: you just let it go. And you let go *to it*, which in writing this story, Rita, you did. Whenever you try to take control, whenever you impose your will, whenever you start thinking your way into this stuff of fiction, not only do you not get control, you lose touch with the very things that are the most important to you and your work. But, you got it. You understood, you assimilated. [Applause.]

Does everybody understand the difference between what happened here and what happened in the examples that were not quite working? Which is not to say that your stories are bad stories, or that you're not as talented as Rita. This is an extremely talented group. Everything I've seen has been impressive in important ways. Don't leave this classroom feeling gloomy or pessimistic or put down. What I've been saying to you this semester is based on my deep respect for your highest ambitions. There are those among you who are capable of creating works of literature that will endure. I've written more bad stuff than you will ever write in your life, and I've wanted to give you a way to measure yourselves from here on out against the very highest standards. Your brand of sumo is not my brand of sumo; I'm just telling you where in yourself to look. I don't want you writing like me or anybody else. That's the whole point. It's deeply personal. It's your brand of sumo.

APPENDIX

"OPEN ARMS"
BY ROBERT OLEN BUTLER

I have no hatred in me. I'm almost certain of that. I fought for my country long enough to lose my wife to another man, a cripple. This was because even though I was alive, I was dead to her, being far away. Perhaps it bothers me a little that his deformity was something he was born with and not earned in the war. But even that doesn't matter. In the end, my country itself was lost and I am no longer there and the two of them are surely suffering, from what I read in the papers about life in a unified Vietnam. They mean nothing to me, really. It seems strange even to mention them like this, and it is stranger still to speak of them before I speak of the man who suffered the most complicated feeling I could imagine. It is he who makes me feel sometimes that I am sitting with my legs crossed in an attitude of peace and with an acceptance of all that I've been taught about the suffering that comes from desire.

There are others I could hate. But I feel sorry for my enemies and the enemies of my country. I live on South Mary Poppins Drive in Gretna, Louisiana, and since I speak perfect English, I am influential with the others who live here, the Westbank Vietnamese. We are all of us from South Vietnam. If you go across the bridge and into New Orleans and you take the interstate north and then turn on a highway named after a chef, you will come to the place called Versailles. There you will find the Vietnamese who are originally from the North. They are Catholics in Versailles. I am a Buddhist. But what I know now about things, I learned from a communist one dark evening in the province of Phu'ó'c Tuy in the Republic of South Vietnam.

I was working as an interpreter for the Australians in their base camp near Núi Đất. The Australians were different from the Americans when they made a camp. The Americans cleared the land, cut it and plowed it and leveled it and strung their barbed wire and put up their tin hootches. The Australians put up tents. They lived under canvas with wooden floors and they didn't cut down the trees. They raised their tents under the trees and you could hear the birds above you when you woke in the morning, and I could think of home that way. My village was far away, up-country, near Pleiku, but my wife was still my wife at that time. I could lie in a tent under the trees and think of her and that would last until I was in the mess hall and I was faced with eggs and curried sausages and beans for breakfast.

The Australians made a good camp, but I could not understand their food, especially at the start of the day. The morning I met Đặng Văn Thập, I first saw him across the mess hall staring at a tray full of this food. He had the commanding officer at one elbow and the executive officer at his other, so I knew he was important, and I looked at Thập closely. His skin was dark, basic peasant blood like me, and he wore a sport shirt of green and blue plaid. He could be anybody on a motor scooter in Saigon or hustling for xích-lộ fares in Vũng Tàu. But I knew there was something special about him right away.

His hair was wildly fanned on his head, the product of VC field-barbering, but there was something else about him that gave him away. He sat between these two Australian officers who were nearly a head taller, and he was hunched forward a little bit. But he seemed enormous, somehow. The people in our village believe in ghosts. Many people in Vietnam have this belief. And sometimes a ghost will appear in human form and then vanish. When that happens and you think back on the encounter, you realize that all along you felt like you were near something enormous, like if you came upon a mountain in the dark and could not see it but knew it was there. I had something of that feeling as I looked at Thập for the first time. Not that I believed he was a ghost. But I knew he was much bigger than the body he was in as he stared at the curried sausages.

Then there was a stir to my left, someone sitting down, but I didn't look right away because Thập held me. "You'll have your chance with him, mate," a voice said in a loud whisper, very near my ear. I turned and it was Captain Townsend, the intelligence officer. His mustache, waxed and twirled to two sharp points, twitched as it usually did when he and I were in the midst of an interrogation and he was getting especially interested in what he heard. But it was Thập now causing the twitch. Townsend's eyes had slid away from me and back across the mess hall, and I followed his gaze. Another Vietnamese was arriving with a tray, an ARVN major, and the C.O. slid over and let the new man sit next to Thập. The major said a few words to Thập and Thập made some sort of answer and the major spoke to the C.O.

"He's our new bushman scout," Townsend said. "The major there is heading back to division after breakfast and then we can talk to him."

I'd heard that a new scout was coming in, but he would be working mostly with the units out interdicting the infiltration routes and so I hadn't given him much thought. Townsend was fumbling around for something and I glanced over. He was pulling a slip of paper out of his pocket. He read a name off the paper, but he butchered the tones and I had no idea what he was saying. I took the paper from him and read Thập's name. Townsend said, "They tell me he's a real smart little bastard. Political cadre. Before that he was a sapper. Brains and a killer, too. Hope this conversion of his is for real."

I looked up and it was the ARVN major who was doing all the talking. He was in fatigues that were so starched and crisp they could sit there all by themselves, and his hair was slicked into careful shape and rose over his forehead in a pompadour the shape of the front fender on the elegant old Citroën sedans you saw around Saigon. Thập had sat back in his chair now and he was watching the major talk, and if I was the major I'd feel very nervous, because the man beside him had the mountain shadow and the steady look of the ghost of somebody his grandfather had cheated or cuckolded or murdered fifty years ago and he was back to take him.

It wasn't until the next day that Captain Townsend dropped Thập's file into the center of my desk. The desk was spread with a dozen photographs, different angles on two dead woodcutters that an Australian patrol had shot yesterday. The woodcutters had been in a restricted area, and when they ran, they were killed. The photos were taken after the two had been laid out in their cart, their arms sprawled, their legs angled like they were leaping up and clicking their heels. The fall of Thập's file scattered the photos, fluttered them away. Townsend said, "Look this over right away, mate. We'll have him here in an hour."

The government program that allowed a longtime, hardcore Viet Cong like Thập to switch sides so easily had a stiff name in Vietnamese but it came to be known as "Open Arms." An hour later, when Thập came through the door with Townsend, he filled the room and looked at me once, knowing everything about me that he wished, and the idea of our opening our arms to him, exposing our chests, our hearts, truly frightened me. In my village you ran from a ghost because if he wants you, he can reach into that chest of yours and pull out not only your heart but your soul as well.

I knew the facts about Thập from the file, but I wondered what he would say about some of these things I'd just read. The things about his life, about the terrible act that turned him away from the cause he'd been fighting for. But Townsend grilled him, through me, for an hour first. He asked him all the things an intelligence captain would be expected to ask, even though the file already had the answers to these questions as well. The division interrogation had already learned all that Thập knew about the locations and strengths of the VC units in our area, the names of shadow government cadre in the villages, things like that. But Thập patiently repeated his answers, smoking one Chesterfield cigarette after another, careful about keeping his ash from falling on the floor, never really looking at either of us, not in the eye, only occasionally at our hands, a quick glance, like he expected us to suddenly be holding a weapon, and he seemed very small now, no less smart and skilled in killing, but a man, at last, in my eyes.

So when Captain Townsend was through, he gave me a nod and, as we'd arranged, he stepped out for me to chat with Thập informally. Townsend figured that Thập might feel more comfortable talking with his countryman one on one. I had my doubts about that. Still, I was interested in this man, though not for the reasons Townsend was. At that moment I didn't care about the tactical intelligence my boss wanted, and so even before he was out of the room I intended to ignore it. But I felt no guilt. He had all he needed already.

As soon as the Australian was gone, Thập lifted his face high for the first time and blew a puff of smoke toward the ceiling. This stopped me cold, like he'd just sprung an ambush from the undergrowth where he'd been crouching very low. He did not look at me. He watched the smoke rise and he waited, his face placid. Finally I felt my voice would come out steady and I said, "We are from the same region. I am from Pleiku Province." The file said that Thập was from Kontum, the next province north, bordering both Cambodia and Laos. He said nothing, though he lowered his face a little. He looked straight ahead and took another drag on his cigarette, a long one, the ash lengthening visibly, doubling in size, as he drew the smoke in.

I knew from the file the sadness he was bearing, but I wanted to make him show it to me, speak of it. I knew I should talk with him indirectly, at least for a time. But I could only think of the crude approach, and to my shame, I took it. I said, "Do you have family there?"

His face turned to me now, and I could not draw a breath. I thought for a moment that my first impression of him had been correct. He was a ghost and this was the moment he would carry me away with him. My breath was gone, never to return. But he did not dissolve into the air. His eyes fixed me and then they went down to the file on the desk, as if to say that I asked what I already knew. He had been sent to Phu'ó'c Tuy Province to indoctrinate the villagers. He was a master, our other sources said, of explaining the communist vision of the world to the woodcutters and fishermen and rice farmers. And meanwhile, in Kontum, the tactics had changed, as they always do, and three months ago the VC made a lesson out of a little village that had a chief with a taste for American consumer goods and information to trade for them. This time the lesson was severe and the ones who did not run were all killed. Thập's wife and two children expected to be safe because someone was supposed to know whose family they were. They stayed and they were murdered by the VC and Thập made a choice.

His eyes were still on the file and my breath had come back to me and I said, "Yes, I know."

He turned away again and he stared at the cigarette, watched the curl of smoke without drawing it into him. I said, "But isn't that just the war? I thought you were a believer."

"I still am," he said and then he looked at me and smiled faintly, but the smile was only for himself, like he knew what I was thinking. And he did. "This is nothing new," he said. "I confessed to the same thing at your division headquarters. I believe in the government caring for all the people, the poor before the rich. I believe in the state of personal purity that makes this possible. But I finally came to believe that the government these men from the north want to set up can't be controlled by the very people it's supposed to serve."

"And what do you think of these people you've joined to fight with now?" I said.

He took a last drag on his cigarette and then leaned forward to stub it out in an ashtray at the corner of my desk. He sat back and folded his hands in his lap and his face grew still, his mouth drew down in placid seriousness. "I understand them," he said. "The Amercans, too. I learned about their history. What they believe is good."

I admit that my first impulse at this was to challenge him. He didn't know anything about the history of Western democracy until after he'd left the communists. They killed his wife and his children and he wanted to get them. But I knew that what he said was also true. He was a believer. I could see his Buddhist upbringing in him. The communists could appeal to that. They couldn't touch the Catholics, but the Buddhists who didn't believe in all the mysticism were well prepared for communism. The communists were full of right views, right intentions, right speech, and all that. And Buddha's second Truth, about the thirst of the passions being the big trap, the communists were real strict about that, real prudes. If a VC got caught by his superiors with a pinup, just a girl in a bathing suit even, he'd be in very deep trouble.

That thing Thập said about personal purity. After it sank in a little bit, it pissed me off. But this is a weakness of my own,

I guess, though at times I can't quite see it as a weakness. I'm not that good a Buddhist. I live in America and things just don't look the way my mother and my grandmother explained them to me. But Thập suddenly seemed a little too smug. And I wasn't frightened by him anymore. He was a communist prude and I even had trouble figuring out how he'd brought himself to make a couple of kids. Then, to my shame, I said, "You miss being with your wife, do you?" What I almost said was, "Do you miss sleeping with your wife?" but I wasn't quite that heartless, even with this smug true believer who until very recently had been a bitter enemy of my country.

Changing my question as I did, even as I spoke it, I thought I would never get the answer to what I really wanted to know. As soon as the words were out of my mouth, I felt a flush spread from under my chin and up my face. It was only a minor attack of shame until I saw what was happening before me. I suppose it was the suddenness of this question, its unexpectedness, that caught him off guard. It's an old interrogation trick. But Thập's hands rose gently from his lap and I knew they were remembering her. It all happened in a few seconds and the hands simply lifted up briefly, but I knew without any doubt that his palms, his fingertips, were stunned by the memory of touching her. Then the hands returned to his lap and he said in a low voice, "Of course I miss her."

I asked him no more questions, and after he was gone, my own hands, lying on the desktop, grew restless, rose and then hid in my lap and burned with their own soft memories. I still had a wife and she had not been my wife for long before I'd had to leave her. I knew that Thập was no ghost but a man and he loved his wife and desired her as I loved and desired mine and that was within the bounds of his purity. He was a man, but I wished from then on only to stay far away from him. The infantry guys had their own interpreter and I wouldn't have to deal with Thập and I was very glad for that.

Less than a week later, however, I saw him again. It was on a Sunday. Early that morning there'd been some contact out in the Long Khánh Mountains just to the east of us. First there was the popping of small arms for a few minutes and then a long roar, the mini-guns on the Cobras as they swooped in, and then there was silence.

In the afternoon the enlisted men played cricket and I sat beneath a tree with my eyes on them but not really following this strange game, just feeling the press of the tree's shade and listening to the thunk of the ball on the bat and the smatterings of applause, and I let the breeze bring me a vision of my wife wearing her aó dài, the long silk panels fluttering, as if lifted by this very breeze, as if she was nearby, waiting for me. And a few times as I sat there, I thought of Thập. Maybe it was my wife who brought him to me, the link of our yearning hands. But it wasn't until the evening that I actually saw him.

It was in the officers' club. Sometimes they had a film to show and this was one of the nights. Captain Townsend got me there early to help him move the wicker chairs around to face the big bed sheet they'd put up at one end for a screen. Townsend wouldn't tell me what the film was. When I asked him, he just winked and said, "You'll like it, mate," and I figured it was another of the Norman Wisdom films. This little man, Wisdom, was forever being knocked down and tormented by a world of people bigger than him. Townsend knew I didn't like these films, and so I decided that was what the wink was all about.

Thập came in with a couple of the infantry officers and I was sorry to see that their interpreter wasn't with them. I couldn't understand why they had him here. I guess they were trying to make him feel welcome, a part of their world. I still think that. They just didn't understand what sort of man he was. They clapped him on the back and pointed to the screen and the projector, and they tried their own few words of Vietnamese with him and some of that baby talk, the pidgin English that sounded so ridiculous to me, even with English being my second language. I didn't think Thập would like Norman Wisdom either. Thập and I were both little men.

But when he came in, the thing I was most concerned about was that since I was the only other Vietnamese in the club, Thập would seek me out for help. But he didn't. He glanced at me once and that was it. The two infantry officers took him up to the front row and sat him between them, and when Thập was settled, my attention shifted enough that I finally realized that something was going on here out of the ordinary. The Aussies were unusually boisterous, poking at one another and laughing, and one of them yelled to Townsend, "You intelligence boys have to smuggle this stuff in?"

Townsend laughed and said, "It was too bloody hot even for us, mate."

I didn't know what he was talking about and I was evidently staring at Captain Townsend with my confusion clear on my face. He looked at me and then put his arm around my shoulders. "You'll see," he said. "It's for all us boys who are missing our little ladies." He nodded me toward the chairs and I went and sat a couple of rows behind Thập and a little to his left. I could see only the back of his head, the spray of his hair, his deep brown neck, the collar of his plaid shirt. He raised his face to the screen and the lights went out and the films began.

There were nine of them, each lasting about twenty minutes. The first began without any credits. A man was walking along a country path. He was a large, blond-haired man, Swedish I later learned, though at the time it simply struck me that this wasn't the sort of man who would be in a Norman Wisdom movie. He was dressed in tight blue jeans and a flannel shirt that was unbuttoned, exposing his bare chest. I had never seen an Englishman dressed like that. Or an Australian either. And Wisdom's movies were all in black and white. This one was in grainy color and the camera was quaking just a little bit and then I realized that all I was hearing were the sounds of the projector clicking away and the men beginning to laugh. There was no soundtrack on this film. Someone shouted something that I didn't catch, then someone else. I thought at first that there'd been a mistake. This was the wrong film and the men were telling Townsend to stop the show, put on little Norman. But then the camera turned to a young woman standing by a fence with cows in the background and she was wearing shorts that were cut high up into her crotch and she shook her long hair and the Australians whooped. The camera returned to the man and he was clearly agitated and the club filled with cries that I could understand now: Go for her, mate; put it to her, mate; get on with it.

I glanced at Thập and his face was lifted to the screen, but of course he did not know what was about to happen. I looked up, too, and the man and woman were talking with each other and then they kissed. Not for long. The woman pulled back and knelt down before the man and she unsnapped and unzipped his blue jeans and she pulled them down and he still had his underpants on. I discovered, a little to my surprise, that I could not breathe very well and I felt weak in my arms. I had never seen a film like this, though I'd heard things about them. But there was a moment, when the man remained clad in his underpants, that I thought there was still some boundary here, that this was not a true example of the films I'd heard about.

But the woman squeezed at him there, playfully, smiling, like this was wonderful fun for her, and then she stripped off his underpants. His body was ready for her and that was very clear there, right on the screen, and she seemed truly happy about this and she brought her face near to this part of him and I drew in a sudden breath as she did a thing that I had never even asked my wife to do, though seeing it now made me weak with desire for her.

And then I looked at Thập. It was simply a reflex. I still had not put together what was happening in this club and what Thập was and what had happened to him in his life and what he believed. I looked to him and his face was still lifted; he was watching, and I glanced up and the woman's eyes lifted, too; she looked at the man even as she did this for him, and I returned to Thập and now his face was coming down, very slowly. His head bowed low and it remained bowed and I watched him for as long as I could.

I must admit, to my shame, that it was not very long. I was distracted. I said before, speaking of Thập's "personal purity," that an indifference to this notion is a weakness of mine. I have never remarried, and I must admit that it pleases me to look at the pictures in some of the magazines easily available in America. The women are so naked I feel I know them very well and the looks on their faces are usually so pleasant that they seem somehow willing for me to know them this way—me personally. It's a childish fantasy, I realize, hardly the right intentions, and I suppose someday this little desire will lead to unhappiness. But I am susceptible to that. And on that dark night, in that Australian tent in the province of Phu'ó'c Tuy, I was filled with desire, and I watched all nine films, desiring my wife—mostly her, I think—but at times, too, briefly desiring one of these long-haired women who took such pleasure in the passing farmer, the sailor on the town, the delivery man, even the elderly and rather small doctor.

Three more times I looked at Thập. The first time, his head was still bowed. The second time, he was, to my surprise, looking at the screen. He was watching as the camera settled on the face of a dark-haired woman who was being made love to in the only way I had ever known to do it, and for a time all we could see was her face, turned a little to the side, jarred again and again, her eyes closed. But on her face was a smile, quiet, full of love, but a little sad, like she knew her man would soon have to leave her. I know I was reading this into her from my own life. She was a Swedish prostitute making a porno-graphic movie, and the smile was nothing of this sort. It was fake. And I know that it's the same with all the smiles in the magazines. The smiles of these naked women are the smiles of money, of fame, of a hope to break into movies or buy some cocaine or whatever. But on that night in the Australian tent, Thập and I looked at this woman's face and I know what I felt and something told me that Thập was feeling that, too. He watched for a long time, his face lifted, his hands, I know, yearning.

He was still watching as I turned my own face back to the screen. There were two more films after that, and I viewed them carefully. But my mind was now on Thập. I knew that a few rows in front of me he was suffering. This man had been my sworn enemy till a week ago. The others in this room had been my friends. But Thập was my countryman in some deeper way. And it had nothing to do with his being Vietnamese, either. I knew what was happening inside him. He was desir-ing his wife, just as I was desiring mine. Except on that night I thought I would one day be with my wife again, and his was newly dead.

But if that was all of it, I don't think he would have made this impression on me that does not leave. These films he saw sucked at his desire, brought the feel of his wife to him, made his hands rise before him. He was a man, after all. I watched the films till there were no more and I felt bad for Thập, his wanting a woman, wanting his wife, his being drawn by that very yearning to a vision of her body as ashes now and bits of bone. The third time I looked at him, his head was bowed again

268 Appendix: "Open Arms" by Robert Olen Butler

and it probably remained bowed. It was bowed still when the lights went on and Captain Townsend was called to the front of the room and was hailed for his show with wild applause and cheers.

And as we all shuffled out of the tent I saw Thập's face briefly, between his two Australian mates, the two infantry officers who had made him feel like he was really part of the gang. Thập's face told me how it would all end. His eyes were wildly restless, like he'd been on a sapper mission and a flare had just gone off and he suddenly found himself here in the midst of his enemy.

That night he went to a tent and killed one of the two infantry officers, the one, no doubt, who had insisted on his coming to the club. Then Thập killed himself, a bullet in his brain. It was lucky for Townsend that Thập didn't understand the cheers at the end or the captain might have been chosen instead of the infantry officer. Thập's desire for his wife had made him very unhappy. But it alone did not drive him to his final act. That was a result of a history lesson. Thập was a true believer, and that night he felt that he had suddenly understood the democracies he was trying to believe in. He felt that the communists whom he had rightly broken with, who had killed his wife and shown him their own fatal flaw, nevertheless had been right about all the rest of us. The fact that the impurity of the West had touched Thập directly, had made him feel something strongly for his dead wife, had only made things worse. He'd had no choice.

And as for myself, I live my life in the United States of America. I work in a bank. I have my own apartment with my own furniture and I have saved more money than I expect ever to need, if I can keep my job. And there's no worry about that. It's a big bank and they like me there. I can talk to the Vietnamese customers, and they think I'm a good worker beyond that. I read the newspapers. I subscribe to several magazines, and in one of them beautiful women smile at me each month. I no longer think of my wife. I go to the movies. I own a VCR and at last I saw the movie "Mary Poppins." The street I live on is one of four named after Mary Poppins in our neighborhood. This is true. You can look it up on any street map.

The Vietnamese on the Westbank do not like the Vietnamese in Versailles. The ones on the Westbank point out that for the ones in Versailles, freedom only means the freedom to make money. They are cold people, driving people, Northerners. The Southerners say that for them, freedom means the freedom to think, to enjoy life. The Vietnamese in Versailles do not like the Southerners. We are lazy people, to them. Unfocused. Greedy but not capable of working hard together for what we want. They say that they are the ones who understand America and how to succeed here. There are many on the Westbank and in Versailles who are full of hatred.

I say that desire can lead to unhappiness, and so can a strong belief. I can sit for long hours from the late afternoon and into the darkness of night and I do not feel compelled to watch anything or hear anything or do anything. I can think about Thập and I can fold my hands together and at those times there is no hatred at all within me.

I JUST KNOW